CRYSTAL
HEALING

CRYSTAL
HEALING

THE PRACTICAL GUIDE TO USING CRYSTALS
FOR HEALTH AND WELL-BEING

SIMON AND SUE LILLY

WATKINS PUBLISHING
LONDON

Crystal Healing
Simon and Sue Lilly

Distributed in the USA and Canada by
Sterling Publishing Co., Inc.
387 Park Avenue South
New York, NY 10016-8810

This edition first published in the UK and USA in 2010 by
Watkins Publishing, an imprint of Duncan Baird Publishers Ltd
Sixth Floor, Castle House
75–76 Wells Street
London W1T 3QH

Conceived, created and designed by Duncan Baird Publishers

Managing Editor: Kirty Topiwala
Editor: Zoë Fargher
Designer: Luana Gobbo
Illustrator: Linda Frichtel
Line artwork: Sailesh Patel
Photography: Simon H. Lilly and Matthew Ward

Library of Congress Cataloging-in-Publication Data available

ISBN: 978-1-907486-31-9

10 9 8 7 6 5 4 3 2 1

Typeset in Ehrhardt and Didot
Color reproduction by Colourscan
Printed in Singapore by Imago

For information about custom editions, special sales, premium and corporate
purchases, please contact Sterling Special Sales Department at 800-805-5489 or
specialsales@sterlingpub.com.

Publisher's note: The information in this book is not intended as a substitute for
professional medical advice and treatment. If you are pregnant or are suffering from
any medical conditions or health problems, it is recommended that you consult
a medical professional before following any of the advice or practice suggested in
this book. Duncan Baird Publishers, or any other persons who have been involved
in working on this publication, cannot accept responsibility for any injuries or
damage incurred as a result of following the information, exercises or therapeutic
techniques contained in this book.

Dedicated to all our teachers,
human and non-human.

CONTENTS

FOREWORD

Rather than a book of explanations and theories, we hope that this will be a book to work with and directly experience. Its purpose is to provide clear guidelines for those who wish to explore the potential benefits of crystal healing for themselves.

Crystal healing works through the interaction of the stones and your body's natural subtle energies. Unlike modern medical treatments, these techniques have no obvious scientific rationale or data. For some, this lack of logic and clear cause-and-effect can be disorienting, particularly when, as in this volume, many of the healing processes do not even involve direct physical contact between human and crystal. We would ask you, the reader, to be an explorer, to take the same stance that we encourage in every one of our new students on crystal healing courses: be alert, be sceptical, but be open to new experience.

Mankind's use of crystals and gemstones has always straddled the gulf that appears to exist between science and magic, practical rationality and poetic imagination. Thousands of years ago crystals were used in magic and ritual as well as for practical purposes such as metal-making and creating pigments. Similarly, in the modern world, the parallel uses of stones for spiritual healing and as popular "good-luck" charms contrast with the vital role they play in our advanced technology. Nothing has changed over the millennia in that regard, except for the emergence of different world-views and belief systems. One great difference from the past is in the accessibility of many more gems and minerals. Crystal collecting was once the quirky hobby of a few gentleman scientists who sourced curiosities from commercial miners. Now it is a huge industry that caters to a fascinated general public.

Our approach in this book has been to present processes and techniques that are as easy as possible to accomplish. There is a natural tendency for people to want to skip the boring basics and proceed directly to advanced areas, imagining these to be more fulfilling and exciting. This is nearly always self-defeating. In crystal

healing, there is no "basic" or "advanced", only what is appropriate or not appropriate for an individual's needs. Time and again we see students impatient to move on to more esoteric, detailed or specialized studies. Soon they realize that, in fact, if they pay attention to what appear to be simple techniques, and develop true awareness of their own practice, profound changes occur, and significant healing can take place without effort.

We have found that the most effective healing happens when the body is not confused with too much energy or information. Each crystal can be thought of as a packet of information or a set of instructions. When someone is confused or lost, simple, concise, clear directions are easier to remember and to follow. Therefore, while the techniques use a wide variety of stones, few procedures in this book involve the use of more than three different types of crystal.

We suggest that you explore those techniques that seem to address your situation and also those that pique your curiosity. If you can, it is best to work little and often on your issues. In this way, you will gradually reduce the stress levels that contribute to so many health problems. You will see that many techniques are related to one another, and we make suggestions for other processes that may be helpful in dealing with different aspects of the same issue.

Our situations in life are complex, and solutions to a problem can also be multi-levelled. There will always be more than one way to deal with a situation, but to make a start in your own healing, to take responsibility for your own life and to move in the direction of your personal goals is a powerful first step.

PERSONAL PATHS TO HEALING

To work well with crystals it is important to understand the holistic approach to healing. Although all human beings are biologically similar, we are each of us unique. In sometimes very small, but often very important respects, our uniqueness affects the ways that we suffer and the ways that we heal.

Difficult situations create hugely varying degrees of stress in each one of us, depending on the different circumstances of our lives. Something that one person will shrug off as a minor irritation will be a major trauma to another. Our personalities are shaped by our weaknesses as well as by our strengths and we learn to cope with life by building up a personal world-view that inevitably contains contradictions and faults of logic. These can put strain on body and mind and are often revealed in repeating patterns of behaviour, life experiences, accidents or illnesses, though they can be difficult to identify in ourselves because we accept them as reality. Where we have the greatest accumulation of stressing factors, where our energies are mismatched the most – that is where symptoms of disease will tend to manifest, as these areas are the weakest parts of our makeup.

Holistic healing addresses the underlying weaknesses that have allowed physical symptoms to arise. To treat the same set of symptoms, one person may require balance at a physical level, while another might find it more effective to work on emotional stress. For true healing of a condition to take place, stress will probably need to be released from several different areas of your being over time.

Like unknotting a big ball of string, or opening a combination lock, for healing to be permanent and effective it must be carried out in the order appropriate to each individual. Sometimes small steps are needed before big issues can be addressed; sometimes work in an apparently unconnected area of the self unexpectedly releases a great tangle of stress.

Regular crystal healing ensures that as much stress as possible is lifted from our energy systems, and prevents its reaccumulation. If we can stop new stresses from settling into our bodies, that helps to focus our self-healing processes on more fundamental, long-term imbalances. The techniques chosen for this book are sometimes directed at specific complaints but are also suitable for everyone because they reduce the overall loading of stress, helping to improve our general well-being.

The first chapter of this book introduces the main concepts and systems that will be referred to throughout. Each of the other five chapters covers an aspect of our lives: our bodies, emotions, life changes, spiritual aspirations and environments.

At the start of each chapter you will find repertories of crystals arranged by colour. These are 40 of our favourite stones, easy to find and broadly useful in all crystal work. (A larger directory with concise information on 100 further crystals is provided at the back of the book.) These stones relate to the theme of the chapter. For example, red and dark-coloured stones have a strengthening effect on the physical systems of the body, so they are placed in the chapter that focuses most on the physical body – Chapter 2: Healing the Body. However, working holistically means working on all levels of the self at once, and these crystals are also broadly useful for all crystal work; the techniques in each chapter use stones of a variety of colours.

There are many ways to work with crystals, and trained crystal therapists can choose from many different approaches to correct an individual's pattern of imbalance. For this book we have drawn on the most appropriate techniques from our long experience in crystal healing and we have selected from those that can be carried out without previous specialized training. The majority are crystal layouts, where specific stones are placed on and around the body. Certain layouts harness the healing properties of colour, and for these exercises it is helpful to use cloths of various colours. Alternatively you can visualize breathing air of the relevant colour for a few moments prior to the exercise. Specialized layouts called "crystal nets", which catch specific types of healing energies and concentrate them around the person being healed, also appear. These nets are unique to our crystal healing method, and their names often refer to the aspects of reality they were designed to explore, which we can only briefly explain in these pages.

Other exercises in this book are visualizations and meditations. A few exercises also suggest the use of dowsing. Many healers use dowsing, often with a pendulum, to quickly access the information available to the unconscious mind. In this way it is possible to determine the status of the individual's energies and find the best way to help. Dowsing is a confirmation, in visible terms, of the accurate intuitive feelings that we all are born with.

We suggest you approach all these techniques with an open mind and try out whichever seem appropriate for you.

CHAPTER 1

THE PAST, MAGIC & BELIEF

Why is it that we associate crystals, the most solid and earthy of substances, with ethereal, heavenly worlds? Are we simply valuing the stability and permanence of stone compared to the ephemeral, emotional turbulence of human existence? What is it that attracts us, just like our distant ancestors, to the dazzling colours and otherworldly shapes of crystals and gemstones? Even in our scientific age, we still hold on to the notion of powerful stones, lucky stones, birthstones. What is it that makes some of us believe, intuitively, that a crystal can cure our bodies, even change our lives?

This chapter introduces you to the science and magic of crystals. You will find information about how crystals form, guidance on accessing the levels of the subtle bodies, techniques for preparation and grounding, and some important basic layouts.

CONNECTING WITH CRYSTALS

If we can put aside the rational, scientific viewpoint that we have come to equate with intelligence and "common sense", and look at the world in a more immediate and sense-oriented way, we can perhaps get an idea of how our ancestors perceived crystals. From this more poetic and magical perspective, when something reminds us of another object we "see" a link, a resonance, a connection between those things. Therefore a crystal sparkling in the darkness has a resonance with the stars in the night sky, a red stone has within it the heat of embers and the energy of blood. The connection is immediate and obvious to the senses. Whereas today we consider such links to be coincidental, in the past they had a valuable significance. This understanding of resonance, the symbolic and associative linking of disparate things by similarities of form or quality, is the very basis of all magical and ritual operations, and at the heart of our relationship with stone.

At deep levels of the mind this way of connecting experiences is natural and immediate. It goes way beyond known facts and, without needing to deny the rational, appeals to our need to see patterns and meaning in the world around us. It mirrors the way the unconscious mind seems to operate – for it is the unconscious mind that runs the body and drives the emotions: the deep mind is the driver, while conscious awareness is at best a back-seat commentator on the view.

We see the process at work in all the traditional associations of gemstones with planets, parts of the body, emotions and illness, and this is still the main way that the qualities of stones are intuited today. Appearance, colour, shape, patterning and occurrence are tangible characteristics that tell the story of what the stone "means".

To science this seems nonsense, but that is because science looks at the world in a completely different way. Just because something is non-scientific does not make it worthless. Science all too easily dismisses the emotions, but without emotional involvement in the world life loses most of its meaning and all of its enjoyment.

Perhaps crystal healing works so well simply because it bypasses the constraints of common sense and satisfies a more basic need for a personal and intimate connection and harmony with the world. It seems to be this connection that we all need in order to maintain our mental stability and physical well-being.

THE RESONANCE OF QUARTZ

Although not an effective way to start fire, quartz pebbles when rubbed or struck together in darkness will generate a faint burst of light. Our cave-dwelling ancestors will have known of this phenomenon. Quartz crystals, and many crystals in general, sparkle with light and colour. Like the stars, they seem to contain light. Stars resemble distant flickering campfires of the spirits. Spirits gather, as humans do, around the warmth of fires; and it is natural that they will gather around the fire of crystals. Stars sparkle in the darkness of the night sky, crystals in the darkness of the earth. Although our dead are put into the earth, the ancestor spirits are in the sky with other spirits. So then, quartz must be a way to link with the spirits of the heavenly worlds and the ancestors. In many cultures quartz crystals are the pre-eminent tools for spiritual knowledge, transformation and healing. They are often thought of as fragments of heaven.

PERFECT IMPERFECTIONS

Crystals are the most organized matter in the universe, the most stable and the most coherent, but they are not quite perfect, and it is this imperfection that gives them their amazing properties.

A perfect system is self-balancing, requiring no input and remaining inert in all situations. The way in which rocks and crystals form rarely allows for such perfection. Superheated gases and liquids deep in the Earth's crust contain many different types of elemental atoms which, under the right circumstances of temperature and pressure, fall out of solution. They begin to settle together in the most "comfortable" way they can. Depending on the type, size and weight of the atoms, different elements will come together in various ways making regular, repeated patterns or "lattices". This regularity can be seen in the planes and faces of a crystal and explains why crystals of the same mineral will always be identical in this regard. What we see is actually the multiplication of the smallest atomic arrangement within the stone.

Atoms of different sizes and elements (such as oxygen, gold, carbon, sulphur) can combine in many ways under different circumstances to make chemical compounds, which when they are solid are called minerals. These minerals can take a very organized form in the correct conditions, making what we call crystals of that mineral. Different minerals crystallize in different conditions, but all arise from a gaseous or a liquid saturated solution filled with a soup of atoms. Carbon, for example, will only form diamond crystals under extremely high temperatures and pressures miles below the surface: it will form graphite when crystallizing at low temperatures. Halite – common salt – forms when the heat of the sun evaporates sea water. Salt mined from the earth is simply salt from ancient evaporated seas.

Most types of crystals used in healing and industry are formed when gases and liquid solutions surge upwards through volcanoes, rock fissures and fractures in the Earth's crust. At different depths, temperatures and pressures change, allowing many varied crystals to form according to the optimal conditions they require. The harder crystals such as ruby, emerald, topaz and quartz form quite deep in the earth. Softer crystals such as fluorite, pyrites and azurite form at lower temperatures and pressures.

The growth of a crystal lattice will be affected by its environment. Even though the lattice structure is regular and the relationship of angles and faces remains constant, more atoms tend to accumulate on one side of the flow than the other, so that perfectly symmetrical crystals are rare. Often different types of minerals will crystallize at the same time, sometimes even inter-growing. It is not known precisely how long crystals take to form in the Earth's crust. However, the process requires very specific conditions that cannot remain the same for long, and so it is likely that crystals form quickly, within small windows of opportunity.

Grown crystals can remain in their original form indefinitely, for thousands, or even millions of years, but they may still be subject to external changes. The same bursts of super-heated fluids that create crystals in the first place can alter or dissolve already existent crystal beds. They can be changed into completely different crystals – by the process known as metamorphosis. Even the prolonged action of water and erosion at the Earth's surface can bring about new crystallizations.

The dynamic creation of crystals in turbulent conditions inevitably means that rogue atoms get caught up in the growing crystal. Most colour in crystals is caused by these interlopers, which even at very low concentrations affect the way in which light passes through the crystal, changing the visible colour. Colour and transparency in a crystal are dictated by whether light photons can pass between the atoms of the lattice, or whether they are bounced back. Opaque crystals reflect all light from their surfaces; translucent crystals distort and bounce back some light; transparent crystals let all light pass through.

HUMANS AND CRYSTALS

The use of crystals in mechanical and electronic technology has long been familiar – for example, to amplify light in lasers, and as conductors in crystal radios. The common assumption that crystals function in a similar way when used as healing tools is rather naïve and not based on any correlating evidence. However, the human system is certainly a conductive electrical entity. Our cells communicate with one another electro-chemically, but also through tiny bursts of light (bioluminescence). Increasingly sophisticated scientific measuring devices are making it clear that our bodies are sensitive to minute fluctuations of any electric field. It is still within the bounds of possibility that, in the healing process, crystals and humans interact as two dynamic equilibriums, exchanging energy information and feedback loops.

17

PRELIMINARIES AND PRECAUTIONS

Holistic healing addresses underlying weaknesses that have allowed physical symptoms to arise. For healing to be effective it must be carried out in the order appropriate to each individual – as if we each have our own inner combination lock. Sometimes small steps are needed before big issues can be addressed; work in an apparently unconnected area of the self can unexpectedly release a great tangle of stress. We can all ensure that as much stress as possible is lifted off our energy systems and prevent accumulations of new stress. This helps to focus self-healing on deeper imbalances. The techniques in this book, especially the energy nets, efficiently reduce the overall stress loading, thus helping to improve our general well-being.

TIPS FOR SUCCESSFUL HEALING

- It is possible to be seated for crystal healing, but it is easier lying down. A yoga mat or blanket on the floor is ideal.

- Wear loose clothing, and remove all bulky and metal items: phones, spectacles, watches and particularly jewelry (which can affect balance procedures). Make sure you will not be disturbed. Have some surgical tape to hand, just in case you need it to keep your crystals in place for an exercise.

- Take plenty of time to relax after a session – as a general rule, wait double the session time before you resume normal activity, as this gives plenty of time for your system to adjust to its new balance. Drink a little cold water.

- Short, regular sessions (5–10 minutes, once or twice a week) are much more valuable for releasing stress and maintaining healthy balance than occasional long sessions.

- Remember that every session is a unique event. Do not expect any particular experience or effect. Unusual sensations and imagery can occur as a result of stress release and readjustment of subtle energy. But a quiet, unremarkable session does not signify that "nothing has happened". It is the end result that matters, not your experiences during the session.

Cleansing your crystals regularly ensures unwanted influences are not transferred to them. You should cleanse your crystals before and after every use.

- Running water: Hold your crystal under running water, and visualize imbalances flowing away. Place in the sun to dry.
- Sound resonance: Place your stones in a singing bowl, or make sound above the crystals with hand cymbals (tingshaws), rattles or bells.
- Purification by smoke: Pass your crystals through aromatic smoke from traditional herbal smudge sticks and incense (sandalwood, sage, juniper, cedar, frankincense, and so on).
- Purification by cleansing spray: Fill a diffuser spray with your choice of flower essence combinations, essential oils, herbal distillates and so on. Spray your crystal, then allow it to dry in the sun.
- Breath and visualization: Hold the crystal and blow forcefully over it while imagining imbalances being blown away.
- Salt or clay: For deep cleansing, pile dry sea salt or clay around a crystal, and leave for 24 hours. Discard the salt or clay afterwards – do not reuse.

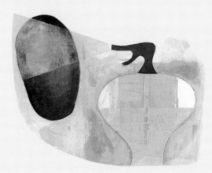

- Crystal clusters: to cleanse small crystals, place them on a larger cluster or bed of crystals, and leave overnight. Useful for cleansing crystal jewelry.

BEING PREPARED FOR UNEXPECTED REACTIONS

Feelings of physical discomfort or emotional turbulence can sometimes occur during healing sessions. These will usually subside by themselves in a few moments. If they persist or become uncomfortable, simply remove the crystals and move away from them until you feel settled. Use grounding stones and centring techniques if required (see pages 20–21). Complete your healing session with a very basic balance, such as the Spectrum Chakra Balance (see page 27), to restore equilibrium.

GROUNDING AND INTEGRATION

These days we often seem to be confronted by a stark choice: between a "spiritual" and a "material" way of life. The new spirituality exhorts us to delve into the fine layers of existence, on the assumption that the more subtle energies we know about, the better and more spiritual we will be. The problem is often that this tends to steer people away from the practicalities of living in the world, making daily life seem boring and lacking in glamour, or else, in the opinion of many established religions, making it seem like some clever trap to prevent us from reaching spiritual goals.

There are also those, however, who encourage us to engage fully with our lives and to embrace the world and its solidity. People of this persuasion tend to favour more grounded ways of living, believing that to really become who we are, we do indeed need to embrace our physical existence. For if our physical body is the focus-point of all levels of our being, then it follows that in ordinary awareness we already have access to all the knowledge of the fine levels, even though we may not be aware of this. What we do not have is a solid experience of physical manifestation. To develop our full potential, therefore, we need to be "here" and "now". Our focus needs to be inward, to fully engage with the centre of our physical presence; and at the same time it needs to be downward, to link into the centre of our world.

If we focus too much on the development of subtle skills and the knowledge of subtle energies without balancing them out by caring for the physical body and developing our practical skills, then the energy balance in the body can easily be upset. The aura becomes top-heavy, with energy concentrated in the upper body and head, leaving little to feed the digestive system, reproductive system and lower limbs. Eventually these areas develop dysfunctions as they suffer from a continual lack of life-energy. This situation tends to be common in urban societies where rational knowledge and logical deduction are valued above intuition.

Our planet Earth is our main source of nurturing energy. Moreover, Earth also provides a safe release-point for excess or unwanted energy. These links to the planet are therefore crucial for our health and well-being. Through crystals we can access these links; we can ground ourselves and keep our energies in balance.

There are a number of crystal placement points called "anchor points". Crystals can be placed on any of these points, but can be particularly effective when three or more anchor points are used in combination. It is rarely necessary or appropriate to use all these points at the same time. Use intuition to select a few. Experiment on yourself to gauge the different effects each placement has. Ideal crystals for grounding are any dark-coloured stones (red, brown, black or metallic). If you use stones with points (terminations), ensure that these are directed down the body (toward the feet or ground), as this will emphasize their grounding and integrating qualities.

THE 10 ANCHOR POINTS

1 Front of the pelvis (hipbones)

2 Centre of the pelvis (pubic bone)

3 Base of the spine

4 On the midline between the legs, at thigh-level

5 The knees

6 On the midline between the calves or lower legs

7 Between the feet

8 On the arch (top) or sole (bottom) of each foot

9 Below each foot

10 On the midline, below the level of the feet

SUBTLE LAYERS

Most cultural traditions have ways to describe our non-physical or subtle bodies. Each system is different. But all subtle systems (chakras, aura, subtle bodies, meridians) are to some extent helpful maps to describe how things really are.

The aura is made up of layers invisible to the external senses. A few of these layers (such as the thermal and electrical) can be measured by scientific instruments, but most can only be sensed by our own inner awareness. Near the body all these levels interpenetrate, becoming more attenuated the further away they are from the physical. The subtle bodies of the aura have been linked to specific qualities (emotions, thoughts, beliefs), although these vary from one tradition to another.

When layers have blocks or shadows, the energy from the universe is unable to flow easily through them to the physical body. This prevents us from being in harmony with ourselves and with our environment. Crystal healing techniques are ideally suited to clearing problems from these layers. Removing blocks from subtle bodies is a proactive approach to long-term health, as well as an excellent way of dealing with immediate problems.

To understand how the subtle bodies work, it helps if we imagine ourselves as a wave on the ocean. Our physical body is the very peak of that wave. Going deeper into the wave itself, we move away from the experience of time and space and the physical limitations of the body and into a broader definition of who we are, our emotions and our thoughts. If we go deeper still, a point is eventually reached where the edges of one wave cannot be differentiated from others: it stops being an individual wave and becomes part of the ocean. Similarly, the finer our levels become, the more we lose our sense of separateness, our individual definition. However, at these levels we also have unlimited access and freedom, as there are no boundaries to prevent free movement of energy between the levels of existence.

Although we may take excursions into the collective layers of consciousness for inspiration or healing, we need to be able to feel secure in our physical bodies to be able to live in the world and to stay healthy. When we move in and out of the deep, collective layers, we must ensure that our personal boundaries remain in place. Without this energy integrity we become open to influences that can destabilize our physical, emotional and mental functioning. Grounding and centring exercises and crystal layouts are effective for securing our personal energy boundaries.

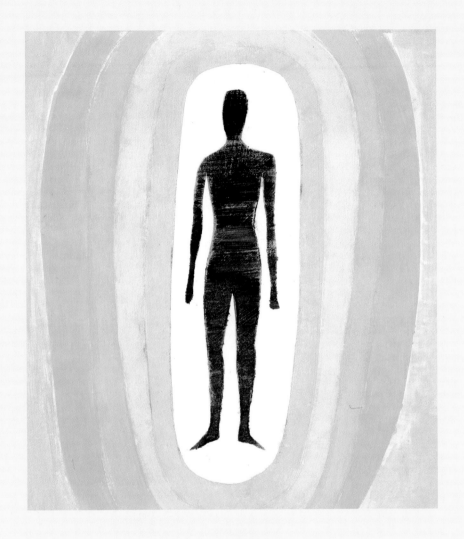

KASHMIR SHAIVISM

In the Hindu philosophy of Kashmir Shaivism the descent into manifestation is visualized as energy emerging from a single point. This occurs through the process of becoming increasingly conscious and aware. Finally, near the very end, the awareness of individuality causes the manifestation of the senses and ultimately the five elements: ether, air, fire, water and earth. Our physical bodies, therefore, are only a small part of what we really are, even though we are unable to investigate the finer layers of ourselves with our ordinary levels of awareness.

UNDERSTANDING THE CHAKRAS

There are several energy maps of the body that are used by crystal healers. Of these the chakra system is probably the most familiar. The first translations of the Vedic philosophies from India introduced the ideas of chakras to the West in the early twentieth century. Translations of important texts by Sir John Woodroffe (also known as Arthur Avalon) were available to the Theosophists (a society devoted to uncovering universal truths through the study of ancient religions and philosophies) from 1913 onward, and the information derived from these texts remained almost entirely within that group until the 1960s.

Since that time the concepts of the chakras and the chakra system have been modified and simplified for use in the West, but this energy map has remained a most useful tool for assessment and for healing.

The system describes six major energy centres located on a central energy channel, and another just above the head, which maintain and reflect the functions of our being at many different levels (see diagram, below). The central channel is situated just in front of the spine and in addition there are two further energy channels weaving across the central channel and across each other. The interaction of all three flowing channels creates the vortices of energy known as the chakras. Each centre has many correspondences to activities, behaviours, emotions, thoughts, colours, shapes, animals, and much more.

It is important to realize that the whole system is interlinked. Although we may identify an imbalance in a certain chakra, that imbalance will probably be affecting all chakras.

In crystal healing we are able to work on releasing imbalances within chakras, but also on ensuring that the chakra system as a whole maintains its optimum functioning to help the body to heal itself.

In the Western system, each main chakra centre has been linked to a colour of the rainbow spectrum, as itemized in the table on the opposite page. This provides an ideal, straightforward format for working with crystals that can be used by anyone.

CHAKRA LOCATION, COLOUR AND ASSOCIATIONS

SYMBOL	CHAKRA	LOCATION	COLOUR	ASSOCIATIONS
	Root chakra	Base of the spine	Red	• energy • groundedness • practicality
	Sacral chakra	Midway between the navel and the pubic bone	Orange	• creativity • sensation • flow • repair • enjoyment
	Solar plexus chakra	Midway between the navel and the diaphragm	Yellow	• personal power • understanding • digestion • confidence
	Heart chakra	Centre of the chest	Green	• relationships • love • balance • space • growth
	Throat chakra	Base of the throat	Light blue	• communication • expression • peace
	Brow chakra	Centre of the forehead	Indigo	• perception • vision • intuition
	Crown chakra	Just above the top of head	Violet, white or gold	• integration • coherence • universal connection

THE MINOR CHAKRAS

Your aura contains thousands of *nadi*s (energy channels), and a chakra forms
each time one *nadi* crosses another, so there are many "minor" chakras
in addition to the main seven. Several are used in exercises in this book,
including the thymus chakra, midway between the throat and heart chakras;
the earth star chakra, the same distance below the feet as the root chakra is
above the feet; the plantar chakras, in the centres of the soles of the feet; and
the palm chakras, in the palms of the hands.

CHAKRA BALANCES

The chakra system is a well-documented framework that can be adapted in many different ways. The two techniques described here are the simplest and are very easy to use. They are often taught as the starting points for any professional crystal therapist training.

The Spectrum Chakra Balance (opposite) is a general, all-body balance that helps to gently smooth out minor energy fluctuations. It reinforces chakra energies, helping them to return to normal functioning. This balance, which you can use on a daily basis as a body-maintenance and support, follows Western colour correspondences – the colours of the rainbow – making it easy to remember. However, there is no "right" or "wrong" colour or crystal choice for any chakra: each chakra resonates to all colours at various levels. The second technique (below) is an adaptation of the Spectrum Chakra Balance, giving you the freedom to follow intuitive choices of crystals.

INTUITIVE CHAKRA BALANCE

Any crystal can be placed on any chakra to balance your chakras according to your immediate needs, so in this layout the colour of crystal chosen is left open to the intuition. Relax and let your inner wisdom guide you to the right stone.

1 Ensure you can see your stones easily. Choose a grounding stone (see pages 20–21) to go between your feet.
2 Take a few deep breaths, close your eyes, and take your attention to your root chakra. Then open your eyes and look at your crystals. Pick up the first stone you notice. This crystal will balance the root chakra.
3 Repeat the procedure for each of the other six major chakras. Place the stones in a line beside where you are going to lie down, so that you can place them easily on your body, starting at the root chakra.
4 Lie down, place your stones on the appropriate chakras, and leave them in place for 4–5 minutes.
5 When you have finished, remove the stones from the head downward.

If you have a wide selection of different crystals, group them into colours before you begin. This will help you to choose a stone easily, by intuition, from each colour.

1 Choose a grounding stone (black, brown or dark red), a red stone, an orange stone, a yellow stone, a green stone, a light blue stone, a small, dark blue stone and a violet, clear or multi-coloured stone. Allow your intuition to guide you to the best stone for balancing each chakra.

2 Place the grounding stone below and between your feet.

3 Place the red stone between your legs, either near the base of your spine or between your knees. Lie down, placing the other stones within easy reach.

4 Place the orange stone midway between the navel and the pubic bone.

5 Place the yellow stone midway between your navel and the bottom of your rib cage.

6 Place the green stone at the centre of your chest, level with your heart.

7 Place the light blue stone at the base of your throat, on the sternal notch.

8 Place the small, dark blue stone on the centre of your forehead.

9 Place the violet, clear or multi-coloured stone on the floor just above the top of your head.

10 Stay still, with the stones in place, for 4–5 minutes.

11 Remove the stones, starting with the one just above the top of the head.

12 Take a few minutes' rest, still lying down, before returning to normal activity.

THE SEAL OF SOLOMON

This healing pattern is one of the original layouts from the early days of modern crystal therapy. Sometimes called "Star of David", it is basically a six-pointed star comprising two intersecting equilateral triangles. In classical and medieval magic and alchemy these triangles symbolized the union of the four elements, fire, earth, air and water, which were conceived as combinations of earthly and heavenly qualities. Perhaps it is no coincidence that the hexagon, made by linking all six points of the star, represents the cross-section of a quartz crystal. It is also found within other natural structures, including corals, bone cells, bee hives, carbon atoms, and so on.

THE SEAL OF SOLOMON

When the points of your crystals (terminations) are directed away from the body, this pattern will release imbalances and clear tension. The points are then turned toward the body to re-energize and restore equilibrium.

1 Select six clear quartz crystals. Place them evenly spaced around where your body will be when you lie down: one at the top of the head; one by each shoulder or upper arm; one by each thigh or upper leg; and one on the midline below and between the feet. Make sure that all the points are turned outward, away from your body.

2 Lie down and stay still for 3–5 minutes.

3 Now turn all your crystals so that the points face inward, toward the body. Lie down again and stay still for a further 2–4 minutes.

You can also use the Seal of Solomon template on smaller areas of the body that need more focused healing. Simply arrange the crystals in the six-pointed pattern in the most convenient places surrounding the target area. Often some stones will be off the body and some placed on the body. You may need some surgical tape to keep some of the crystals in place. Adding an extra central stone can help to focus the healing action in an appropriate way. To select this stone, refer to the crystal repertories at the beginning of each chapter, or go to the directory at the back of the book. Or, from your crystal set, select a stone of the most applicable colour, using the following guide:

- RED – energizes
- ORANGE – soothes
- YELLOW – clarifies
- GREEN – calms
- BLUE – quietens
- INDIGO – eases flow
- VIOLET – integrates
- PINK – reduces aggravation
- WHITE – cleanses
- BLACK – quietens and grounds

INWARD OR OUTWARD?

Often a clear difference can be felt according to whether your crystals are turned inward or outward. If there is any discomfort, simply reverse the direction of the stones: discomfort caused by the crystals will then quickly disappear. This shows that sometimes it is necessary to perform the "charging" process, with the points of the crystals turned inward, before the "releasing". With this technique it is best to follow the sequence that feels more comfortable for you.

FIVE-LINE CLEARING

Five-line Clearing is one of the most popular and the most versatile of our own specially devised techniques. It is ideal for all sorts of healing work and can be done by anyone as it requires no conscious knowledge of the true state of the individual and needs no interpretation. Unfortunately, it is not possible to use this process directly on yourself, but it can be modified for self-treatment, by using the hand as a microcosm of the body (see box, page 50).

The technique was designed as a simple way to introduce a moving crystal into the auric field around the body and, in this way, create a dynamic healing effect, which quickly dispels blocks and imbalances in the subtle levels of consciousness. Key to this is the use of a free-swinging crystal pendulum which can react to each situation in unique ways.

SETTING YOUR INTENTION

Before starting the clearing it is necessary to set the healing parameters with a clear intention, expressly stating this to yourself. Initially, it is a good idea to make a very full, clear intention: that "the pendulum will move out of its neutral swing whenever it identifies an imbalance that can be removed quickly, safely and appropriately, and once done, will return to its neutral swing".

Because the method works on every level of energy, you can set a very broad intention (for example, "to remove any imbalances that are quick, safe and appropriate to deal with at this time") or a very specific one ("to reduce the symptoms of X and Y", or "to reduce the stress associated with Z").

Carry out the procedure calmly and let the crystal do its work – you will not know precisely what problems are being addressed, or on what level the clearing occurs.

In this exercise a free-swinging crystal pendulum reacts to imbalances in the subtle bodies, gently removing them in order to restore a smooth flow of energy.

1 You will need a quartz crystal attached to a thread, or contained within a metal spiral attached to a thread. Different crystals will remove different stresses. Clear quartz has the most general applicability in balancing and clearing. Other quartz (smoky, amethyst, citrine, rutilated, tourmaline) will also be effective. Other minerals will often have a much more tightly focused action (as suggested by the colour and qualities).

2 Ask the person you are healing to lie down comfortably on his or her back.

3 Imagine that their body is divided by five vertical lines: the midline (line 1), crossing their navel, from below the feet to above the head; two lines parallel to this (2 and 3), up their legs to their shoulders and past each side of their head; and two outer lines (4 and 5) beyond the outside edge of their physical body.

4 Kneel alongside them and hold the crystal pendulum in a relaxed hand. Set it into a neutral swing: a straight line back and forth in line with your own forearm.

5 Move the pendulum slowly up the midline of the body (line 1) from beneath their feet, maintaining this neutral swing. Where there are areas of imbalance the crystal is able to remove, it will diverge from the neutral swing in some way. When this happens, relax and hold your position until the neutral swing returns.

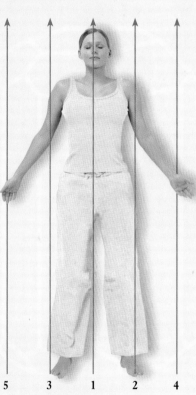

6 Continue up the line, allowing the pendulum to rotate or move in any way whenever it begins to leave the neutral swing.

7 When you reach the top of the head, move to the lower end of the next line (line 2). Repeat the process until all five lines have been cleared. Remember to cleanse the pendulum after you have finished.

31

CHAPTER 2

HEALING THE BODY

In crystal healing, the body is seen as the central focus where many different expressions of personal energy are located in one place. Illness and disease always indicate the presence of underlying imbalance and stress acting on an individual. Physical symptoms may only be the final, visible stages of a problem that has remained hidden for a long time. Illness is thus like the shadow of an original problem, cast from another place. A shadow cannot be "cured" (although its cold, dark influence can be lessened). The object casting the shadow must be removed: only then will its influence disappear.

The techniques in this chapter will help you to identify the causes of pain and illness, and reduce the stresses that prevent your body from repairing itself. There are often many possible approaches to healing a physical problem, so remain open-minded, and experiment with the exercises shown here.

BLACK TOURMALINE
(Complex aluminium borosilicate)

KEYWORDS: Grounding, protecting
- *Realigns body structure*
- *Deflects negativity*

SMOKY QUARTZ
(Silicon dioxide)

KEYWORDS: Beginnings, stability
- *Energizes the body*
- *Calms the mind*

Tourmaline is found in every colour. The black variety is sometimes called "schorl". When black tourmaline is translucent, it may have a brown or dark green tint. It deflects many types of harmful energy, and can be worn on the body or placed in a space for protection. This crystal works with your core structure, easing muscles and aligning the skeleton. It can also help to align a person or space with the energy of the planet. Black tourmaline has a stabilizing effect on the physical, mental and spiritual levels of being. It is an excellent grounding stone, helping to anchor the physical and subtle bodies into the planet.

Smoky quartz is found in mountainous or volcanic regions. The colour,which can vary from a very pale, transparent grey to a solid, opaque black, is thought to have been caused by low levels of natural radiation. Smoky quartz is linked to the root chakra and has an energizing effect on the physical body while being quietly grounding. This crystal slows down the thought processes, creating tranquillity of mind and reducing the impact of disturbances from the outside world, making it a valuable meditation aid. It can also help to expand the subtle senses and makes an excellent support for divination or channelling.

HAEMATITE
(Ferric iron oxide)

KEYWORDS: Establishing, grounding
- *Energizes the body*
- *Anchors life-energy*

OBSIDIAN
(Complex silicate with inclusions)

KEYWORDS: Cleansing, transforming
- *Releases trapped feelings*
- *Grounds body and mind*

Haematite's high iron content makes even a small crystal surprisingly heavy. The mineral is usually found in rounded lumps with shiny, metallic surfaces, though weathered surfaces are powdery and red. It is a brittle stone and will shatter if dropped onto a hard surface. Haematite is said to protect against harm from invisible spirits. For most people, its effect is grounding and stabilizing, though for a small minority it has the opposite effect, creating a dreamy state of mind. Linked to the root chakra, haematite boosts self-esteem, bringing strength and courage. Its iron content also supports the flow of life-energy around the physical and subtle bodies.

Obsidian forms in rapidly cooling lava flows. It is technically a non-crystalline glass, because it lacks a crystal lattice. Its colour varies from a translucent pale grey (these stones are known as "Apache tears") to a dense, shiny black. This crystal has sharp edges, which made it a useful material for tools in ancient cultures, and a highly reflective surface, often polished to create mirrors. Obsidian breaks down barriers to access and cleanse our deepest emotions. Grounding and protecting, this crystal is linked to the root chakra and to minor chakras beneath the feet. It can also improve the functioning of the digestive system.

MAGNETITE & LODESTONE
(Ferric and ferrous oxides)

KEYWORDS: Aligning, grounding
- *Releases stress*
- *Energizes subtle bodies*

JASPER
(Silicon dioxide with inclusions)

KEYWORDS: Restoring, anchoring
- *Encourages practicality*
- *Aids problem-solving*

Magnetite forms large magnetic masses and is the main source of iron ore. Lodestone is the name given to magnetite that demonstrates a magnetic polarity; it often has a rougher surface than magnetite, with attached magnetized fragments (above, left). Both stones help us to stay in harmony within ourselves and with the outside world by keeping us grounded and attuned to the electromagnetic energies of the planet. They align our chakra and subtle energies so that we become internally centred, feel more vital and release stress. These two crystals can also help to determine appropriate spiritual direction in life.

Jaspers show huge variation in pattern and colour. Red jasper is the most common type (above, right); other jaspers are named depending on their appearance or the location where they are found. Bloodstone ("heliotrope"), is green jasper with red spots (see also page 133). Ocean (or orbicular) jasper has green, blue and cream concentric patterns. Light jasper with black spots is Dalmatian jasper, while the spotted yellow variety is called leopardskin (above, left). All jaspers are grounding, especially the brown and red varieties, and they all encourage problem-solving. The individual varieties bring additional qualities linked to their chakra colour (see page 25).

GARNET
(Complex aluminium or calcium silicates)

KEYWORDS: Activating, stimulating
- *Promotes energy flow*
- *Boosts energy levels*

Garnets are complex, variable mixtures of minerals which produce several different colours, from rich red to opaque green and transparent orange. All garnets are activating and increase energy levels, making them helpful when beginning new projects. They will also help to heal illnesses linked to cold or damp, and break patterns of inertia. However, the colour of a garnet will determine the exact focus of its healing. Red garnets provide powerful boosts of energy, so are best used for short periods of time or mediated with clear quartz. Orange garnets are warming and encourage a smooth flow of energy. Green garnets are gently activating and supportive.

RUBY
(Aluminium oxide)

KEYWORDS: Nourishing, steadying
- *Brings confidence and security*
- *Boosts enthusiasm for life*

Ruby is a variety of the mineral corundum, coloured by chromium oxides. It is extremely hard, and can be scratched only by diamond. Rubies form characteristic octagonal crystals, which are usually cut into cross-sections. When the stone has rutile inclusions, it is cut into domes to create star ruby. Ruby is associated with the sun and is thought to bring health and wealth. It radiates a constant, sustaining energy that feels warm and secure. Linked to the heart chakra, ruby encourages feelings of self-worth and self-esteem. It can create and sustain a positive flow of energy between people, and so can be used to heal relationship problems.

ALIGNING BONES AND MUSCLES

We think of our skeletons as being rigid and unchanging, but in fact they are living structures that adapt to and alter with our circumstances. Our bones provide protection for the soft internal organs as well as attachment points for muscles, and movement and support for the whole body. It's therefore not surprising that structural problems and misalignments in our musculo-skeletal system can cause a great range of problems. If the balance of muscle and bone is lost even in one small area, this can lead to discomfort and dysfunction in several other places, as the body attempts to compensate and regain equilibrium. Tissues, organs, nerves and blood supply can become compressed or distorted, affecting their functioning. Repetitive action, poor posture, stress and infection can all contribute to structural problems. The layouts below and on the opposite page will help re-establish a balanced and aligned deep structure.

ALIGNING THE SPINE

Your vertebrae should be able to move independently of one other so that your spine can remain flexible and balanced. Physical and emotional stress can lock bones together, resulting in physical weakness and a lack of energy. This technique helps to relax and settle your skeleton, and so is an effective treatment for a bad back. It can also help ease pulled muscles and headaches, and clarify muddled thinking.

1 Select a clear quartz crystal or any other brilliant, clear stone (such as apophyllite, danburite or Herkimer diamond). Lie down in a comfortable position on the floor.

2 Place the crystal at the centre of your forehead.

3 Relax. As you breathe in, imagine that you are drawing in a bright light through the stone right into the centre of your brain. Exhale and repeat.

4 Continue for a few minutes and then relax. You may notice an increased clarity of mind or sense of relaxation. Repeat when necessary.

The grounding energies of the eight black or dark green tourmalines of the Earth Net will help the body readjust to its correct structural alignment.

Black tourmalines × 8

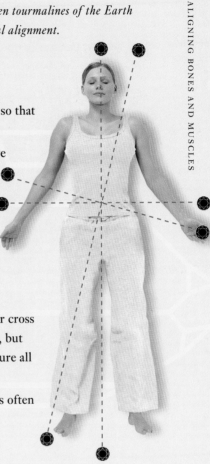

1 Spread out a green cloth on the floor, arranged so that when you lie down, your head will point north.

2 Place a tourmaline stone on the cloth, just above where your head will be when you lie down.

3 Place a second crystal on the midline just below where your feet will be.

4 Place a tourmaline either side of where your body will be, level with your navel. This makes a cross of four stones aligned to the cardinal directions.

5 Place the next four tourmalines to make another cross with the same centre and the same proportions, but about 10–20 degrees clockwise of the first. Ensure all the stones are pointing toward the body.

6 Lie down in the net for 6–10 minutes. Repeat as often as required.

OTHER STONES FOR TREATING BONES AND MUSCLES

COPPER MINERALS such as malachite, turquoise, chrysocolla or native copper ore are excellent for relieving muscle pain and inflammation.

RUTILATED QUARTZ will speed the repair of damaged muscles.

CLEAR QUARTZ placed either side of your head, close to the bottom of your ears, will ease jaw tension.

DIAMOND placed near the top of the skull is the best way to realign the bones of the skull and jaw, and will help to relieve head and neck aches as well as sinus problems.

EASING HEADACHES AND INSOMNIA

Headaches and insomnia are common problems that sometimes become serious, chronic conditions. They are difficult to treat because the causes are so varied. Headaches are usually produced by abnormal blood flow to the brain. Physical tension is often the root cause, because it leads to misalignment of the spine, neck and jaw, and muscular imbalances that restrict blood flow. Relaxing and easing muscular tension often helps and, happily, the many small muscles of the scalp, jaw, face and neck are fairly responsive to crystal placement. Insomnia – the prolonged inability to get sufficient sleep – is also often caused by tension, so similar techniques can be effective. Digestive problems, the result of incorrect or unbalanced nutrition or food intolerances, can also cause insomnia, and are sometimes related to the most debilitating headaches of all: migraines.

Regular sufferers of these problems should try to keep stress levels manageable with key crystal healing layouts (see pages 28–31) and practise regular grounding as well as the settling and soothing layouts explained on these pages. These techniques should be used as a preventative measure: do not wait for headaches to strike before you act.

BROW CHAKRA TEMPLATE

This simple layout balances the brow chakra, helping to ease eye strain, headaches, confusion and restlessness.

1 Select a lapis lazuli or Herkimer diamond, three fluorites of any colour and a fourth of blue or indigo. Lie down in a comfortable position on the floor.

2 Place a lapis lazuli or Herkimer diamond on the centre of your forehead.

3 Place a fluorite on either side and one above the central stone, close to your hairline. If you wish, you can place the blue or indigo fluorite on the floor a short distance above the crown of your head.

4 Relax for 4–5 minutes, then remove the crystals. Repeat every 2–3 days.

SETTLING LAYOUT

The quietening, soothing crystals used in this layout will calm agitation and restlessness, particularly of the mind and nervous system.

Smoky quartz × 1

Carnelian × 1

Serpentine × 2

Amethyst × 1

1 Place the smoky quartz on the midline just below where your feet will be when you lie down.

2 Lie down in a comfortable position. Place the carnelian on your lower abdomen.

3 Place a serpentine stone at the centre of your chest, over your heart chakra.

4 Place a second serpentine stone at your throat, over your throat chakra.

5 Finally, place the amethyst above your head.

6 Stay in this position for 5–6 minutes, then remove the stones. Repeat whenever you feel the need.

LONG-TERM SOLUTIONS

To ease headaches and insomnia more permanently, sufficient energy needs to be anchored into the body and excess energy released. Grounding stones can be of great benefit in this process. Place stones such as amethyst, black tourmaline, staurolite or chrysoprase below the feet or in any of the anchor point positions (see pages 20–21). For insomnia, stones can also be kept close to the sleeper during the night in small bags safety-pinned to the mattress, or placed on the floor beneath the bed. (N.B. never put small stones loose in children's or babies' beds: tie them into bags and ensure they cannot be removed or swallowed.)

ACTIVATING CIRCULATION AND DIGESTION

The health of your circulatory and digestive systems relies on maintaining their smooth flow. Both systems allow nutrients to be absorbed by the body. Digestion breaks down food by mechanical and chemical means, enabling the absorption of useful molecules by the blood for distribution in the body. Blood also picks up oxygen as it passes through the lungs, pumped by the heart and contraction of muscles. These systems are also the means of elimination: the blood clears toxins and waste from organs via the kidneys, and the gut expels waste matter, dead cells and toxins.

A great many factors can upset these two systems. Stress and tension can cause muscles to tighten, leading to restricted or sluggish blood flow. Poor diet, or a lack of physical movement or appropriate exercise can reduce the efficiency of these vital processes.

The warming energy of ruby in the Sun Net, opposite, can be used to stimulate and maintain your circulatory and digestive systems, and keep things moving. Other techniques in this book are also worth experimenting with to optimize these areas: the Moon Net (page 47), the Sacral Chakra Template (page 142) and the Etheric Body Net (page 105).

RED STONES FOR VIGOUR AND PROTECTION

Traditionally, red stones are linked with blood, and thus with vitality, life-force, protection from harm and safety in battle. Bloodstone, a green jasper with flecks of red, was thought to stem the loss of blood from injuries, making it popular with soldiers. Haematite, a powdery red oxide of iron weathered to clay-like red ochre, not only has blood's colour but also its metallic smell. Known as "the blood of the earth", for centuries haematite was a powerful material traded over thousands of miles. Red gemstones such as spinels, garnets, rubies and zircons were often chosen as the central stone on royal crowns owing to their protective qualities.

Ruby is associated with the sun, the centre of the solar system, and the heart, the centre of the body. Its red colour is naturally activating and will gently stimulate the circulation of all forms of energy. The Sun Net will stimulate and encourage the functions of assimilation and elimination in a balanced manner. If you would like to energize other areas of stagnant activity in your life, this net can help.

Ruby × 6

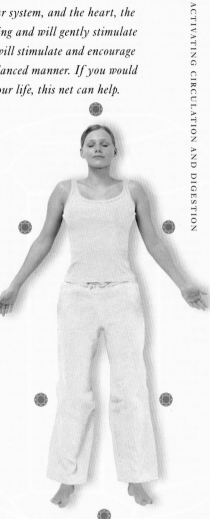

1 Spread out a yellow cloth on the floor. Arrange your crystals on the cloth so that when you lie down, one will be above your head, one on the outside of each elbow, one on the outside of each knee, and one on the midline below your feet.

2 Lie down and remain relaxed in the net for 4–5 minutes.

3 Repeat regularly, whenever you feel in need of more stable energy, or that your life-energy needs revitalizing.

N.B. *You can use low-grade ruby crystals for this exercise, often available as hexagonal, flat slices. Unlike gem-quality rubies, these are relatively inexpensive, but they provide the same sustained, reliable fire energy.*

TREATING DIGESTIVE COMPLAINTS

Digestive upset can be simply but effectively treated with a single stone placement on the solar plexus, just above the navel. A crystal placed in this position will help to soothe tension and ease constriction. Any of the following stones can be useful: aventurine, malachite, moonstone, amethyst, citrine, rose quartz, clear quartz.

ENERGIZING THE BRAIN AND NERVOUS SYSTEM

The nervous system is the major communication network within the body. If the energy required to maintain it is not flowing correctly, we may experience either a dull sluggishness and an inability to focus, or an excessive agitation and mental confusion. Irritability and mood swings can indicate that there is an internal friction upsetting the body's energies or that an energy block in the nervous system is preventing the normal easy flow of nerve signals from one part of the body to another. The gems used in the exercise on the opposite page are gently warming and comforting, and have the power to give a boost of organic energy to an over-burdened nervous system. They will naturally lead to a more permanent positive mood if used over time, as well as helping to calm a digestive system troubled by nervous anxiety or over-sensitivity to certain food groups.

AMBER AND JET

Amber and jet are both organic minerals derived from trees. Jet is fossilized conifer wood, found in many places around the world but most notably along the northeast coast of England. Amber is the fossilized pine resin of ancient forests, buried millions of years ago. Historically, amber's main sources were the Baltic and North Sea coasts, although it is now found in many places worldwide. Both amber and jet are soft, light and easily worked, and have therefore been used for thousands of years to create objects used in ritual and ceremony. They can be polished to a high degree, and when rubbed on some materials will build up a static charge that will attract small pieces of cloth, hair or paper. This characteristic reflects the gems' magical and metaphysical link with the electrical systems of the body, and to the "powers of attraction" of the sun and moon, which in medieval times were thought to draw toward them plants and animals, as well as the tides, and even the souls of the dead.

Amber and jet have a gently stimulating and warming effect. This layout will help to clear imbalances by increasing the flow of energy, even when the imbalance is caused by excess energy in one area. If you find that the warmth of this layout is uncomfortable, try other layouts that use blue, cooling stones instead. These will reduce the "heat" and improve circulation of energy. Alternatively, consider replacing this warming, solar amber and jet layout with a cooling, lunar layout of moonstone (see page 47).

Jet × 1   Amber × 4

1 Place the piece of jet just below where your feet will be when you lie down, on the midline of your body.

2 Lie down and place one amber near the base of your spine, between your thighs (exact placement is not important here).

3 Place the second amber above the top of your head.

4 Hold the two remaining pieces of amber in the palms of your hands. Relax for 3–5 minutes, then remove the stones. Repeat this technique whenever you feel the need.

5 If you have excess nervous energy, this layout may make you feel a little agitated at first. If your discomfort does not ease, repeat the layout with a grounding stone (see pages 20–21) below and between your feet instead of the jet.

MAINTAINING HORMONES AND SKIN

Our hormones and skin are systems that organize, sustain and define our nature. Hormones are chemical messengers that deliver a continual flow of signals around the body, ensuring harmony and co-ordinated reactions. These signals modify our behaviour, fertility, sleep cycles, the growth and maintenance systems of the body, and significantly influence our emotional responses. The skin, the body's largest organ, is a physical boundary separating and protecting us from the outside world. It regulates our body temperature, manufactures Vitamin D and functions as a major sense organ. Through the skin, we define our personal territory and recognize our appearance – "who we are".

Mistaken reactions by the body to certain stimuli, such as pollen or chemicals, exacerbated by stress, can trigger imbalances in both skin and hormones, leading to problems including auto-immune diseases and allergies. Both skin and hormones are associated with the solar plexus chakra, whose major role is organizing our energies to maintain internal power and control. Moonstone and quartz, used here, will help you feel more comfortable within yourself.

PALE YELLOW NET

This simple energy net will enhance your sense of inner and outer harmony.

1 Select six clear quartz crystals. Spread out a yellow cloth on the floor, arranged so that when you lie down, your head will be pointing north.

2 Arrange five quartz crystals on the cloth, so that when you lie down one will be above your head, one just beyond each shoulder, and one just outside each foot. All the stones should point north (up your body).

3 Lie down within the stones. Place the sixth and last crystal on your solar plexus, also pointing north.

4 Remain in this position for 5–6 minutes. Repeat daily if you wish.

MOON NET

Moonstones connect to the energy of tides and the inspirational energy of the moon. Use this net in times of emotional turmoil, or to relieve digestive or hormonal upset.

1 Select five moonstones and spread out a blue cloth on the floor. Lie down on the cloth and arrange the five stones touching your body as follows: one on each hip bone, one on each shoulder, and the fifth on the floor above your head. (Secure the stones with some surgical tape if necessary.)

2 Rest in the net for 5–6 minutes. Repeat as often as necessary to restore balance and gain relief.

STABILIZING THE BREATH

Breathing is the one automatic bodily function that we can easily modify at will. Sustained focus on the breath requires concentration, which is why breathing techniques are a tool in all kinds of physical, mental and spiritual training, including martial arts, yoga and meditation.

Every cell in our bodies requires a constant supply of oxygen to function effectively. The respiratory and circulatory systems (see page 42) work together to transport oxygen to the cells and remove carbon dioxide to be eliminated via the lungs. The mechanical action of the lungs and diaphragm, together with the abdominal muscles, draws fresh air into the body and expels the old. A variety of factors, including muscular tension, can restrict the efficacy of this process, as can infections and allergic reactions that prevent oxygen absorption from the lung surfaces. The crystal work on these pages will help balance and free your breathing.

TECHNIQUE FOR EASY BREATHING

This is a combined crystal layout and visualization that will help to free up the breath and stimulate ease of personal expression.

1 Select three pieces of chrysocolla. Lie down, and place one chrysocolla at the base of your throat. Place the remaining two crystals either side of your rib cage (secured with surgical tape if necessary).

2 Breathe normally. As you breathe in, imagine the breath entering your body through your skin. As you breathe out, visualize the breath leaving your body along the midline, and being drawn down into the ground.

3 Continue the visualization for a couple of minutes, then let it go, and just relax for a further 5–6 minutes with the stones in place. Remove the stones, and repeat whenever you feel the need.

HEART CHAKRA TEMPLATE

This layout stabilizes and balances the heart chakra, benefiting the related physical and emotional systems and bringing spiritual peace. It will ease any sense of weight, restriction, agitation, guilt or sorrow.

Rose quartz × 1   Green tourmaline × 4   Smoky quartz × 4

1 Lie down and place a rose quartz at the centre of your chest, over the heart chakra.

2 Arrange four green tourmalines (or clear quartz points) above, below and to the left and right of the central stone.

3 Place the smoky quartz stones between the tourmalines to form a ring of eight crystals regularly spaced around the central stone. Ensure all stones are pointed away from your heart. (This close arrangement of nine stones is represented by just one icon in the diagram.)

4 Stay in the layout for 4–5 minutes, then remove the stones. Repeat as often as required.

SPACE AND FREEDOM LAYOUT

The following layout can be useful in any situation where you feel under pressure and constricted physically or emotionally, and will ease shallowness of breath.

1 Select five pieces of moss agate (or tree agate). Lie down in a comfortable position. Place a stone at the centre of your chest, over your heart chakra.

2 Place one stone on each side of the central stone on your chest.

3 Place a fourth stone above the central stone, midway between the throat and the heart chakra, at the thymus chakra.

4 Place the fifth agate near your stomach, just below your rib cage on the centre-left of your abdomen. (Secure the stone with surgical tape if necessary.)

5 Rest for 4 to 5 minutes, then remove the stones. Repeat whenever you like.

DETOXIFYING THE BODY

Purification is the aim of all spiritual practices. The removal of what you no longer need from your physical and subtle bodies, but also from your emotions and ideas, allows a clearer experience of ourselves and the world around us. These days the term "detox" mostly describes cleansing the physical body of impurities to lose weight and regain health. In crystal healing, detoxification is a holistic process, removing stress and stressors from all levels of the physical and subtle bodies, in order to encourage the body's own cleansing functions. When the body is functioning well, it rids itself of unwanted substances through normal elimination processes, but periods of intense activity or poor nutrition can interfere with these systems. The deep rest achieved in crystal healing will improve your ability to detox effectively. Here we look at some specific techniques that can aid the process.

HERKIMER CLEANSING

This technique is useful whenever your body feels burdened with the results of over-indulgence, and also when people and situations are having a negative influence over your life. Herkimer diamond is a brilliant double-terminated quartz, excellent for cleansing the body at every level. It can be used as a healing pendulum, placed within a metal spiral attached to a strong thread. (The metal spiral is desirable because it leaves the crystal's terminations uncapped.) You can also use the pendulum to perform Five-line Clearing (see pages 30–31) on a companion. For your own use, the simplest technique is to pass the pendulum over the hand, which can be seen as a microcosm of the whole body. Simply divide your non-dowsing hand vertically by five imaginary lines and pass the pendulum slowly along each line, stopping to release blocks wherever the gem diverts from its usual swing.

SULPHUR DETOXIFICATION

This layout harnesses the cleansing qualities of sulphur and focuses healing on the sacral chakra, the chakra most associated with purification processes.

Smoky quartz × 1

Sulphur × 1

Clear quartz × 1

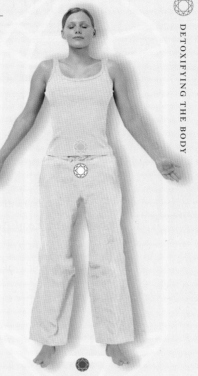

1 Place a smoky quartz below and between where your feet will be when you lie down, to ground and anchor the cleansing process.

2 Lie down and place a small piece of sulphur on your lower abdomen, over the sacral chakra. Just below it, place a clear quartz crystal, pointing toward your feet.

3 Stay in the layout for 3–4 minutes per session, then remove the stones. Repeat every 3–4 days as required. Remember to increase your water consumption to aid the detoxification process.

FINE LEVEL ONE NET

This net amplifies the effects of other crystal nets, and increases clarity. It is a deceptively simple process that has a profound effect on many levels of the self, encouraging cleansing from the centre of your being.

1 Select three smoky quartz crystals and spread out an orange cloth on the floor. Lie down and arrange the stones, points downward, in a triangle: one on the pubic bone (the lowest point on the front of the pelvis), and the other two stones slightly higher, on the groin, where the legs meet the torso.

2 Stay in the net for no more than 4 minutes, then remove the crystals. As waste products and toxins are eliminated from your body, you may experience symptoms such as fatigue, nausea and headaches. Drink sufficient water and take plenty of rest. Do not repeat this net for at least 4 days, to allow time for its effects to work through the system.

DEALING WITH INFERTILITY

The causes of infertility vary widely. As with many health problems perceived to be purely physical in nature, there are often hidden chemical, emotional or hormonal factors that, dealt with carefully, can help the body to repair itself and increase the chances of a successful conception. Emotional stress linked with a lack of fulfilment and low self-worth concentrates in areas of the body related to reproduction; thus, lifting this stress is often a useful first step. These three crystal healing techniques will help to heal the underlying stresses that can affect fertility at the emotional, psychological and subtle levels of the body.

CRYSTAL GARDEN MEDITATION

This meditation can be used any time that you experience feelings of worthlessness, failure, loneliness or isolation.

1   Select five to ten small crystals of any colour and sort. Use your intuition to choose those stones that most appeal to you.

2   Place the crystals around you, anywhere you feel is appropriate.

3   For the next five out-breaths, simply allow yourself to relax.

4   Imagine walking through a small wooded area on a bright spring day. In front of you is a grassy clearing. Lie down on the grass, and feel the sunshine on your face. Feel the energy of the earth beneath your body, pulsing with life.

5   Imagine the crystals around you transforming into spring flowers. Visualize more flowers sprouting beneath you and growing through your body. Feel the sun and the soil feeding the flowers. After 4–5 minutes, allow the flowers to be absorbed into your body.

6   Allow the visualization to fade and then rest for 2–3 minutes before resuming normal activity. This exercise can be repeated daily, if you wish.

VENUS NET

This net links to the energy of the planet Venus, which has long been associated with creativity, fertility and nurturing. The placement of crystals will also help to stimulate artistic expression and improve relationship issues.

Rose quartz × 3   Clear quartz × 2

1 Spread out a green cloth on the floor (if you don't have a cloth this colour, imagine inhaling green light for a minute before you begin).

2 Place a rose quartz on the top of each foot, between the tendons of the first and second toes. (You may need some surgical tape to hold them in place.)

3 Lie down on the cloth and place a rose quartz at the base of your throat.

4 In each hand hold a clear quartz, points directed away from your body.

5 Stay in the net for 5–6 minutes, then remove the stones. You can repeat this net daily if you wish.

PALLAS ATHENE NET

This energy net uses the nurturing colour pink and clarifying energy of quartz to access the powerful protective, maternal and creative aspects of Goddess energy.

1 Select eight clear quartz crystals and spread out a deep pink cloth on the floor (if you don't have a cloth of this colour, while you lie in the net visualize yourself filling your body with dark pink air as you inhale).

2 Place the quartz crystals, points outward, as follows: one above your head, one between your feet, and three arranged evenly on each side of your body.

3 Lie down and stay in the net for 5–6 minutes. Repeat every few days until your sense of self-empowerment improves.

ENHANCING IMMUNITY
AND WELL-BEING

For correct nutritional and immune function, we rely on the body's ability to distinguish between useful and harmful substances. If the identification processes of the digestive or immune system are flawed, problems arise: either toxic substances build up in the body, or necessary nutrients cannot be identified and absorbed. Malnourishment can also occur when the food we consume is inherently unbalanced: modern farming methods deplete soil nutrients, and the levels of vitamins in most farmed food are much lower than 30 or 40 years ago.

The ability of the body to repair itself and withstand infection depends upon its access to a store of nutrients to replace those used in everyday maintenance; if these are inadequate, our immune system weakens. The crystal work on these pages helps to redress the balance. The layout below stimulates natural healing processes, while the Chiron Net, opposite, uses the colour yellow, which encourages the identification and assimilation processes of the body, together with turquoise, which protects and aids healing.

ACTIVATING SUBTLE HEALING LAYOUT

This layout uses peridot (also known as olivine), one of the best crystals for stimulating the energies of the body to release toxins and activate subtle healing.

1 Select four pieces of peridot and a grounding stone. Place the grounding stone on the midline below where your feet will be when you lie down.

2 Slip a peridot under each side of your back so that it is near each kidney. Place a stone at the centre of your chest, over the heart chakra, and one at the base of your throat.

3 Lie down and stay for 3–4 minutes, then remove the peridots but keep the grounding stone in place for a few moments more. You can repeat this layout daily, if you wish.

CHIRON NET

Chiron is a small planetoid that has an eccentric orbit, crossing the paths of both Saturn and Uranus. It is named for the centaur Chiron, the great healer and teacher of Greek heroes including Achilles. Chiron has become associated astrologically with healing and self-integration, particularly of deep levels of hurt. This net can help to clear away blockages left over from the past. It will strengthen personal life-force, supporting your fight against harmful external influences.

1 Select six turquoise stones and spread out a yellow cloth on the floor. Arrange the crystals so that when you lie down, one will be below and between your feet, one on each side of the thighs, close to the hands, one either side of the shoulders, and one above the head. Lie down in the net and settle yourself.

2 Remain in the net for 6–10 minutes. Remove the stones, and take your time to return to normal activity. Repeat daily, if you wish.

CHAPTER 3

BALANCING THE MIND

Our emotions define who we are as much as our bodies do. How we feel moulds our body's attitude, posture and appearance. We tend to distinguish between our mind and our emotions, as if our logical, rational abilities were separate from our impulsive, instinctive reactions. In reality they are inextricably linked, with our "rational" minds constantly occupied in analyzing and justifying our emotional responses.

The most immediate result of crystal work is a quietening of these thought processes, which leads to clearer decision-making and helps to identify the body and mind's most important needs so that healing can take place. The techniques in this chapter are designed to tackle sensitive issues such as depression and addiction, as well as to bring renewed compassion and security.

CARNELIAN
(Silicon dioxide)

KEYWORDS: Repairing, creativity-
enhancing
- *Releases stress and trauma*
- *Gently energizes*

Carnelian (or "cornelian") is
one of the best all-round healing
stones. A variety of quartz known
as chalcedony, it is formed from
mineral solutions coloured by iron.
Carnelian is valued for its deep
orange colouring, and has been used
for centuries in carvings, seals and
jewelry, the latter thought to give the
wearer courage and protection from
harm. Carnelian is closely linked to
the sacral chakra. It gently warms
and restores the flow of energy where
it has stagnated or become blocked.
This stone also releases stress and
trauma that has been locked into the
body, and effectively heals breaks
in the subtle layers. Carnelian also
encourages creativity and relaxation.

CITRINE QUARTZ
(Silicon dioxide)

KEYWORDS: Comforting, uplifting
- *Increases confidence*
- *Activates the intellect*

Natural citrine quartz is relatively
rare, and forms when quartz
crystallizes with inclusions of iron.
The stone can be so pale that it
resembles smoky quartz, but the best-
quality citrine is a pale transparent
yellow. It can be created artificially
by heating amethyst, and this heat-
treated citrine often has a milky-white
base. Whatever its source, citrine
quartz provides a sustaining energy
that is restful and warming. Linked to
the solar plexus chakra, it stimulates
body and mind and activates the
sacral and root chakras, helping to
focus your actions into the present
moment and thereby bring about
success. Citrine is also used to help
increase confidence and self-worth.

RUTILATED QUARTZ
(Silicon dioxide with rutile inclusions)

KEYWORDS: Restoring, linking
- *Accelerates healing*
- *Clears confusion*

COPPER
(Copper ore)

KEYWORDS: Integrating, smoothing
- *Reduces inflammation*
- *Enhances energy flow*

Sometimes called "Venus' hair", this clear or smoky quartz is embedded with long, thin strands of rutile (titanium oxide). These brown, straw-yellow or orange filaments act as rapid transmitters of energy that is then amplified by the purifying quality of the surrounding quartz. Rutile crystals may look metallic but, when held up to the light, reveal a rich red colouring. Rutilated quartz helps to heal any breaks occurring in the subtle energy bodies, because its properties encourage the binding together of elements that help injuries to heal. This leads to an increased flow of energy, which helps to remove blocks to spiritual progress and lift the emotions, even in the darkest of times.

Naturally forming, or "native" copper is rare, and so this mineral is usually extracted by industrial processes. It was named after the island of Cyprus, where the Romans first mined the metal. According to legend, Cyprus was also the birthplace of Venus, which explains her association with copper. Copper helps to maintain an unrestricted flow of energy that can ease inflammation, release tensions and alleviate frustration. It is therefore a natural healer of conflict. It has a beneficial effect on the workings of the brain, clarifying thought processes and improving co-ordination. Copper also helps to resolve disruption caused by opposing astrological and cosmic influences.

59

CALCITE
(Calcium carbonate)

KEYWORDS: Soothing, calming
- *Relaxes body*
- *Quietens thoughts and emotions*

SUNSTONE
(Complex aluminium silicate)

KEYWORDS: Warming, encouraging
- *Stimulates positivity*
- *Encourages creativity and confidence*

Calcite is composed of calcium carbonate, the same mineral from which sea creatures build their shells, eventually forming layers of chalk on the ocean floor. It is a soft stone with a warm, slippery feel, and internal fracture planes that allow it to split easily into regular rhombohedral pieces. Calcite can vary in colour from red to black. The organic spirals of seashells and their watery environment epitomize the qualities of this stone, which enhances the effortless flow of energy through the body and aura to release stress and tension. Calcite also removes unnecessary rigidity, friction and dissonance from our lives, creating a sense of stability and coherence.

Sunstone is a variety of the common mineral feldspar. This crystal gets its name from the iridescent flecks of golden-orange, caused by smaller crystals of iron minerals, that enliven its opaque creamy coloured surfaces. Good-quality sunstone has a delightful warm radiance that helps to encourage a positive outlook on life. Its iron content helps to introduce a down-to-earth, practical motivation to all activities. Sunstone is linked to the sacral and solar plexus chakras, bringing confidence, vitality and creativity, particularly during periods of self-doubt or sadness, or simply when we are in need of sustaining, warming support.

AMBER

(Fossilized organic resins)

KEYWORDS: Enlivening, stimulating
- *Lifts energy levels*
- *Soothes and focuses the mind*

Amber is coniferous tree resin that fossilized more than two million years ago. Although not technically a crystal (it lacks an internal lattice), amber has been considered precious for millennia. It varies in colour from deep, dark brown to a bright lemon yellow, and is soft enough to be worked with sandpaper, melted or moulded. Amber is lightweight and easily becomes charged with static electricity. It stimulates any slow, cold, under-active condition. Linked to the solar plexus chakra, it alleviates conditions linked to the nerves, as well as digestive problems. Amber sharpens the focus of the mind, and helps to swiftly cut through confused thinking and fantasizing.

PYRITE

(Iron sulphide)

KEYWORDS: Activating, cleansing
- *Eases worries*
- *Protects against harm*

The word "pyrite" derives from the Greek word for fire, *pyr*. Pyrite is a soft, brittle stone that produces sparks when struck, and so has been used to make fire throughout history. Its superficial similarity to gold ore gives pyrite one of its other names, "fool's gold" (it is also known as "iron pyrites"). Pyrite links to the sun and the solar plexus chakras, providing warm energy to lift deep gloom, anxiety or frustration. It clarifies the mind and improves memory, perception and the ability to make decisions. Its high sulphur content makes pyrite cleansing and protective against negative influences. It is gently grounding and is therefore often the crystal of choice for sensitive souls.

BUILDING SELF-CONFIDENCE

Self-confidence is the deeply held belief in yourself and your abilities, linked to the qualities of self-esteem, self-assurance and assertiveness. We tend to become less confident during adolescence, often as a result of criticism or negative reinforcement. In adulthood, lack of self-confidence can manifest itself as self-doubt, mistrust of our personal abilities or judgment, and a poor sense of self-worth. These negative feelings can steadily erode our levels of life-energy and, over a period of time, sow the seeds of ill-health. Regular use of simple crystal layouts and wearing of appropriate crystals can help to redress the imbalances at the root of a lack of confidence, and bring a positive, renewed sense of self.

MENTAL CLARITY LAYOUT

This layout is useful if you are confused regarding yourself or a situation that you have found yourself in. The clarifying properties of quartz and beryl will clear up any ambiguities and bring your focus back to your personal needs, making this crystal arrangement particularly helpful if you feel overwhelmed by the strong opinions of others.

1 Select a yellow beryl (heliodor) and two clear quartz with points. (If you don't have a yellow beryl, then a pale yellow citrine point will also work well.) Place the yellow beryl on the centre of your forehead. If your stone has a point, it should be directed upward, away from the body.

2 Place a clear quartz on the inside of each of your wrists (secure them with surgical tape if necessary). Direct the points toward the palms of your hands, away from the rest of your body.

3 Relax and breathe normally. Imagine that your breath is entering and leaving the body through the stones.

4 Remain in the layout for 4–6 minutes. Repeat whenever you feel the need, until you have attained the desired clarity of mind.

SELF-ESTEEM LAYOUT

This layout uses stones that stabilize the energy of the body while allowing energy movement at the solar plexus chakra, which is related to self-esteem. The diopside helps to clarify the boundaries that exist between yourself and others, and also between the idea you have of yourself and the person you truly are.

Smoky quartz × 1   Rose quartz × 1   Diopside × 1

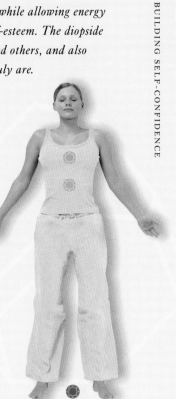

1 Place a smoky quartz below and between your feet. If it has a termination, point this away from the body.

2 Lie down and place a small rose quartz at the centre of your chest, over the heart chakra.

3 Place a piece of diopside midway between the navel and the base of your rib cage, over the solar plexus chakra.

4 Remain in the layout for 3–6 minutes. If you find that emotions begin to well up, take your attention to the smoky quartz at your feet until those feelings subside.

5 Repeat once a day until your self-esteem improves.

STONES FOR SELF-CONFIDENCE

Wearing crystals at your throat, thymus or heart can help to engender self-confidence and assurance. Kunzite, aquamarine or blue lace agate are the most useful crystals to wear at the throat. Turquoise, citrine or carnelian can be used at the thymus. Watermelon tourmaline, rhodocrosite, rhodonite or labradorite are best for use at the heart. Sugilite, charoite, tugtapite, eudialite or ruby in zoisite can be worn to inspire confidence at work or within groups of people. Whatever crystal you choose to wear, ensure that you also carry a grounding stone with you (such as black tourmaline, haematite or smoky quartz) so that any build-up of anxiety can be safely released.

CHALLENGING FEAR AND ANXIETY

Fear can range from mild anxiety to mind-numbing panic, with many stages in between. When it is allowed to become overwhelming, fear is unproductive and can even be dangerous, because its presence impedes you from weighing up information and analyzing the likely success of different strategies. When faced with danger, animals do not think, but act immediately to protect themselves. Their bodies react instinctively to threat, as do ours: diverting blood and oxygen away from non-essential processes to boost the supply to the muscles and brain, and releasing hormones.

Anxiety and fear are the products of a sense of lack of control over our surroundings. In today's complex, technology-driven world, we are routinely confronted with situations over which we have little or no influence. Research has shown that it can be the actual feeling of powerlessness that damages our health. Fear is a problem of the mind and emotions, and one that we can overcome with the right techniques. These procedures will help stabilize the mind and regain perspective on troubling or frightening situations.

FIVE-POINTED HARMONY

The name of the layout opposite derives from its resemblance to the pentagram, or five-pointed star. In early Celtic art, the pentagram was often combined with iconography suggestive of druidic power, which may explain why the pentagram was sometimes labelled the "druid's foot" in medieval literature. Used in medieval times as a protective sign, the pentagram represents the ability to hold, control and direct energy through knowledge and will-power. In China, it symbolizes the five elements (earth, wind, fire, water and ether) from which all matter derives.

This layout links your perceptive mind (via the brow chakra) with your powers of control (represented by the hands) and your powers of action (represented by the feet) to help relieve fear and anxiety.

Grounding stones × 5   OR   Red-coloured stones × 5

1 Choose your stones according to the precise effect you desire. Grounding stones such as black tourmaline, haematite or smoky quartz will quieten the mind. Red, energizing stones such as garnet, zircon or iron quartz will invigorate the body and re-establish your confidence to cope with and overcome difficulties.

2 Lie down and place five stones of the same type in the following layout: one in contact with the outside edge of each foot; one at the centre of the forehead; one in the palm of each hand. Direct any points outward.

3 Remain in position for 5 minutes. Repeat daily for 3 days. If feelings of fear or anxiety persist, repeat daily for a further 4 days. Alternatively, try an extended version of the layout: create a second pentagram outside the first, with five of the same balancing stone such as Herkimer diamond, selenite or kunzite. These stones will dissolve persistent imbalances in your energy field.

TECHNIQUES FOR INTRACTABLE WORRY

A yellow or golden stone placed on your solar plexus chakra will also help to ease a state of worry or anxiety, by increasing your self-confidence, sense of control, assessment skills, and ability to relax. You can also use grounding techniques to reduce mental chatter and calm the body (see pages 20–21).

TRANSFORMING ANGER

Anger is characterized by a build-up of tension that is unable to be equalized or stabilized. Beginning as irritation and annoyance, a repeated stimulus causes friction or aggravation. It impinges on our awareness and disrupts some aspects of the body's natural functioning, overlaying our energy field with a foreign pattern that disrupts order.

This build-up is experienced as a sensation of heat and pressure, increasing and increasing until, as anger, it finally discharges itself to try to restore equilibrium. This natural release process is exacerbated by attempts to suppress it, which only make the pressure greater and the inevitable emotional explosion out of proportion to the original irritant. Internalized over a long period of time, anger creates huge physical stress as pressure is held in check. This stress affects the body's organs and systems, fuelling illness and creating dysfunction. Like an underground fire, anger can smoulder for years before breaking to the surface. These exercises will help to transform angry states before they cause irreparable damage.

PLUTO NET

This net releases the trapped tension that may lead to anger in a gentle but persuasive manner, increasing available life-energy while preventing the build-up of harmful pressures. Obsidian helps hidden aspects of the personality find positive expression, a characteristic it shares with the astrology of the planet Pluto.

1 Select five dark obsidian stones and spread out a black or red cloth. Place a stone on the midline above where your head will be when you lie down.

2 Place one stone on either side of your neck, on an imaginary diagonal line between your ear and the edge of your shoulder

3 Place one stone next to the outside edge of each foot.

4 Lie down in the net and stay for 6–10 minutes, or until the emotions or stress you wish to release have subsided. Repeat daily, if required.

This layout uses the uplifting qualities of citrine and garnet at the solar plexus chakra to combat feelings of vulnerability and powerlessness. Use this layout to defuse a build-up of anger, or to increase positivity in your outlook.

Citrine × 3   Stone of your choice × 1   Garnet × 3

1 Lie down. Place the three citrines, points directed outward, in an upward-pointing triangle between the ribcage and the navel.

2 In the centre of this triangle place a single stone of tiger's eye, ruby, garnet, jasper or pyrite.

3 Place the three red garnets in a downward-pointing triangle around the other stones.

4 Rest here for 4–5 minutes.

5 Remove the stones and place a grounding stone between the feet for 2 minutes. Repeat as necessary.

CHAKRAS FOR RELEASING ANGER

Restoring balance to the chakras (see pages 26–7), in particular the root and solar plexus chakras, is key to releasing anger. The root chakra helps to ground and dissipate the build-up of excess energy, and to combat fear. The solar plexus chakra is also a primary site for addressing the anger state and it is here that issues of control of personal power and maintenance of order are dealt with. Other chakras are also often involved. In young children anger is usually a simple expression of thwarted enjoyment, which is a sacral chakra response. The heart chakra can also be important, especially when anger is the result of an imposition on personal space and personal feelings. As the central point of the whole system, the heart also helps to calm aggravated states.

CALMING OVERSENSITIVITY

Oversensitivity is caused by a lack of grounding and poorly defined personal boundaries. Being insufficiently grounded results in a weakening of our sense of personal security, which can lead to anxiety and vulnerability to external influences. It also means that the body finds it difficult to discharge excess energy, so we may lose our equilibrium under even low levels of stress.

Having unclear boundaries causes oversensitivity to our surroundings, and this tends to affect our whole system. On a physical level we may suffer from food intolerances and allergies, while on an emotional and mental level we might experience extreme fatigue or agitation, confusion in crowds, intolerance of strong emotions in others, and an inability to think clearly. The Saturn Net (opposite) will protect your aura from harmful outside influences, encouraging stability and strength, while the layout below supports grounding and vitality.

RETURN OF STRENGTH LAYOUT

The mixture of green and red in bloodstone makes it ideal for increasing vitality (red) while keeping your personal space balanced (green). Together these two colours support and strengthen our actions and our energy.

1 Select five pieces of bloodstone. Lie down and place the stones as follows: one between your legs, close to the base of your spine; one at the centre of your upper chest between your throat and heart chakras (thymus chakra); one beside each ear; and one at the centre of your forehead.

2 Stay in the layout for 5–6 minutes, then remove the stones. Repeat whenever you need determination, focus or strength, and particularly if you need to reassert your right to personal space.

The energies of the planet Saturn are linked to measured behaviour, discipline and determination. Saturn energies also bring perseverance in the removal of obstacles. Clear and rose quartz combine grounded practicality with clarity, helping you to find constructive ways to overcome problems, and the sturdiness to withstand external pressures without being affected by oversensitivity.

Rose quartz × 4   Clear quartz × 4

1 Spread out a pink cloth on the floor (if you don't have a cloth of this colour, visualize yourself breathing pink-coloured light for a few moments before you begin). Place two rose quartz stones on each foot: one between the tendons of the first and second toes, and one between the tendons of the second and third toes. (Secure the stones with surgical tape if necessary.)

2 Lie down and place a clear quartz on the midline of your pubic bone (the lowest bone of the mid-pelvis).

3 Place a second clear quartz at the centre of your forehead.

4 Hold the remaining quartz crystals, one in each hand. Direct any points downward, toward your feet.

5 Relax in this net for 6–10 minutes, then remove the stones. Repeat as often as you like, whenever you are feeling oversensitive.

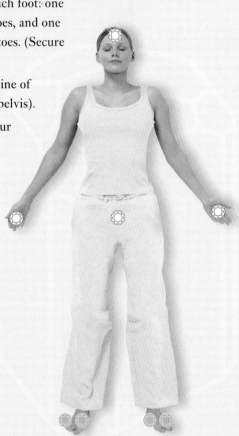

EXPANDING LOVE AND COMPASSION

In many traditions, love and compassion are considered to be the highest spiritual values that we can aspire to. Yet these are concepts that can be hard to define, and seldom do we take a close look at what they really signify. Both qualities are often visualized as radiating from the heart, thereby placing them on the level of feeling rather than intellect. Love and compassion can be thought of as expressions of many positive virtues – for example, understanding, acceptance, tolerance, care, harmony and non-judgment. Feelings of love and compassion support positive, life-affirming action and a feeling of belonging to a nurturing whole. The pink, red and white stones used here are dynamic and unifying. They work to neutralize negativity and aggression, freeing you to be your most loving and compassionate self.

COMPASSIONATE ENERGY NET

This quietening net of clarifying quartz and warming ruby corrects any narrowness in your perception of the value of your actions and purpose in life. It will give you a broader, more accurate understanding of other people and their needs.

1 Select twelve clear quartz crystals and one ruby, and spread out a white cloth on the floor. Place the quartz crystals, points outward, on the cloth, one just above where the top of your head will be, one below your feet, and five evenly spaced on each side of your body.

2 Lie down within this arrangement, and place the ruby at your heart chakra, in the centre of your chest.

3 Stay here for 5–10 minutes. If you wish to clarify your relationship with other people, imagine your breath entering and exiting your body through the ruby. Repeat as often as required.

This net of rose quartz nurtures your personal energy field, to speed up healing and help you direct compassion toward yourself. It will clear away harmful energy, whether the source is internal or external, and will ease feelings of isolation.

Rose quartz × 12

1 Spread out a pink cloth (preferably a strong, dark pink shade) on the floor.

2 Place a rose quartz just above where your head will be when you lie down and one on the midline below where your feet will be.

3 Lie down and space out the remaining crystals as evenly as possible between the first two, five on either side of your body.

4 Relax in the net for 6–10 minutes. Repeat daily until you feel some relief.

BEYOND SELF AND OTHER

Selfish actions are often thought of as inimical to love and compassion. But it's rare for our actions to be entirely altruistic – even our desire for the happiness of others is selfish, because we feel diminished by others' suffering. If we can expand our perspective and become aware that what we experience as personally relevant also affects those around us, we can begin to act for the benefit of all beings without denying our own needs. The self, in other words, expands to include the "other", so that in the end there is no "other". These two crystal nets help to break down some of these artificial divisions, opening you up to the unifying potential of life.

DEALING WITH DEPRESSION

The loss of sense of self, of who we are and the place we occupy in the scheme of things, is something most people experience from time to time. When such feelings persist and become difficult to lift, then a sense of heaviness, dullness and futility can pervade life, increasing feelings of isolation and finally leading to depression. Without the ability to draw sustenance from our surroundings into our aura, we feel diminished, and everything seems to lose its colour and meaning. In the past, treatment for serious depression involved spiritual retreat, practical work, and exercises that required physical and mental discipline. Nowadays chemical intervention is more usual, which can, in fact, perpetuate the problem by creating a greater dissociation of our emotions from the world. Isolation in itself is damaging to your health. The "will to live" is our will to share, support and be a part of the world around us. The exercises on these pages will help to restore this sense of connection.

CROWN CHAKRA TEMPLATE

This template will help whenever you feel a sense of weight, darkness or emptiness in life. These are times when your links to the universal flow of energy may be reduced and you are unable to receive a full measure of this sustaining force (sometimes called "grace"). The clearing properties of quartz can also help to reduce confusion in the mind and improve physical and mental balance and co-ordination.

1 Select three clear quartz crystals. Place the first stone on the midline above where your head will be; place the other two either side of it. If the stones are terminated, then make sure the points are directed outward.

2 Lie down in the layout and relax for 3–4 minutes. If you feel a little unfocused afterward, use grounding stones (see pages 20–21). Repeat as required.

In many ancient religions, the Milky Way was seen as a sacred heavenly river that nourished the spirit of mankind with the forces of creation. The gods and ancestors were said to abide in the stars of the Milky Way – the road to heaven. One earthly manifestation was thought to be the river Nile. The qualities of the crystals and the coloured cloth act together in this net, allowing you to access the energy of the Milky Way. This net will link you to your own ancestral past, helping you to reconnect when you suffer from isolation, dislocation and loneliness.

Smoky quartz × 2   Turquoise × 1   Carnelian × 2

1 Spread out a white cloth on the floor and sit down.

2 Place one smoky quartz in contact with the outer side of each of your feet and then lie down, placing the turquoise at the base of your throat.

3 Hold a carnelian in each hand.

4 Relax and stay in the net for 6–12 minutes, then remove the stones. Take your time before returning to normal activity. Repeat regularly until any difficult feelings ease.

FINDING SECURITY

When we connect our individual energy patterns with the supporting energy of the planet, we become anchored into a larger reality and so regain a clear perspective on our situation, boosting our sense of security and strength, helping to calm fears and anxieties, and releasing unwanted tensions and stresses. Visualizing the Earth Star before crystal healing secures our energy and increases our receptiveness to the subtle effects of crystal nets and layouts, while doing so afterward helps to prolong the benefits of a healing session.

EARTH STAR VISUALIZATION

The Earth Star Visualization will reconnect you to the timeless, deeply stabilizing energy of the Earth.

1 Stand with your feet shoulder-width apart. Take a deep breath. Relax as you breathe out and take your attention down to the base of your spine.

2 Imagine a bright light at the base of your spine and with the next three breaths allow it to become brighter.

3 Take your attention down to the sole of your right foot and imagine a bright light at its centre. With the next three breaths allow it to become brighter. Repeat this process with the sole of your left foot.

4 Imagine lines of light travelling between the base of your spine and the soles of your feet. With the next four breaths, mentally trace these energy lines.

5 Imagine the light at the base of your spine is reflected the same distance below your feet as the base of your spine is above your feet.

6 Breathe in and visualize energy travelling from the base of your spine to your right foot, then from there to the light below your feet and then back up to your left foot and returning to the base of your spine, in a diamond shape.

7 Continue this breathing and visualizing for a couple of minutes, then slowly allow your breathing to return to normal and the visualization to fade.

CONNECTING WITH THE EARTH STAR

This visualization focuses our attention on the subtle energy centres concerned with physical and psychological stability. The root chakra at the base of the spine and our whole existence relies on this strong, firm foundation. Other minor chakras at the soles of our feet, known as the plantar chakras, ensure that our energy system is able to discharge any excess energy. Finally, the earth star chakra, located beneath our feet wherever we are, is a powerful site that integrates individual consciousness with the deep ecology of our planet.

BREAKING HABITS

The problem with repeating patterns in our lives is that they quickly become inevitable habits, rather than personal choices dealt with on an individual basis. A habit is simply a choice that has become locked into place through repetition. Once this occurs, it is no longer really a choice at all. The pattern we repeat becomes part of what we consider our fundamental character or personality, which we do not change.

There is a clear neurological basis for habit. Every action sets up a pathway in the brain for nerve impulses to follow. Once set, these impulses will favour established pathways rather than creating new ones. Thus, a habit "feels right", because it is following an established pathway, regardless of whether it is the best action or not. Biologically, this is an economical and efficient way to establish successful routines of behaviour. However, it can become a problem when the habits are damaging, leading to failure rather than success. It takes considerable effort to change destructive habits, but it can be done by paying attention at the point in time when a different choice can be made. These crystal healing techniques give us a wider perspective on ourselves and our lives, helping us to break negative patterns.

CLARIFYING HEART'S DESIRE

The heart chakra is associated with personal direction, choice and way of life. Working at the heart chakra can therefore help clarify your feelings and encourage decisions that strengthen rather than diminish your personal energy. Lie down and place a green tourmaline (verdelite) at the centre of your chest. Surround it with six clear quartz crystals, with any points directed outward. Stay here for 3–6 minutes. Placing

a Herkimer diamond below the verdelite will increase your ability to achieve goals. Repeat as required.

So called because it is commonly found by roadsides, the Wayfaring Tree is a small tree with a long, flexible trunk, large leaves and white flowers. Our ancestors used this tree to weave baskets, from which we draw its association with memory and repetitive action. Lapis lazuli brings insight and clarity. This will help to improve your awareness of when you make choices that lead you down the wrong paths, and access the deepest levels of your memory, so that you can identify moments when choices have been available that perhaps you weren't aware of at the time.

Lapis lazuli × 6

1 Spread out a red cloth on the floor. Place a lapis lazuli on top, on the midline just above where your head will be when you lie down, and one below where your feet will be.

2 Place another stone on either side of your body, level with where your lower forearms will be, and one on either side of your body, level with where your mid-thighs will be. This should form a six-pointed star pattern (hexagon) of lapis lazuli.

3 Lie down in the net and relax for 5–6 minutes.

4 Repeat every 4–5 days until you begin to notice an increased sense of freedom and adaptability.

GOING BACK TO THE SOURCE

Placing Preseli bluestone at the brow chakra is a particularly powerful way of calling to mind the circumstances from which habit patterns arose. You may become aware of incidents early in your life, or even of a scenario in another time and place. Whatever the circumstances, awareness of the origins of habitual behaviour can help to clarify why the same mistakes are repeated and lead to a new, more conscious effort to change. If you don't have any Preseli bluestone, lapis lazuli also works well.

OVERCOMING ADDICTION

Sometimes repeating patterns of behaviour (see pages 76–7) are not checked, even though they are clearly having a negative effect on an individual's life. If unwillingness to let go of that behaviour becomes inability, then some form of addiction is present. Addiction can adopt many forms, some obvious, some subtle. Some addictions are used as ways to escape from life's daily difficulties, others are ingrained patterns that come to be considered as part of someone's persona and without which they would feel a sense of personal loss. Such obsessions can satisfy desires for continuity and structure, but can be profoundly damaging. Not letting go, fixating on the behaviour as a necessity and rationalizing that need keep the situation locked into a negative cycle. These exercises help to create a positive and confident energy, which can help you to muster the extreme strength it will take to relinquish an addictive habit.

NEPTUNE NET

The planet Neptune is associated with obsession, addiction and being lost in imaginary states. The Neptune Net, working through crystals of calcium carbonate which enhance the smooth flow of physical and mental energy, will help you to remove these negative tendencies while giving you inspiration and a new sense of freedom.

1 Select sixteen pieces of calcite, aragonite or chalk (these are all calcium carbonate minerals), and five pieces of smoky quartz. Spread out a blue cloth on the floor, and arrange the calcite, aragonite or chalk on top, evenly spaced around where your body will be placed.

2 Place a smoky quartz crystal between the first and second toes of each foot. Point the stones away from your feet and secure them with surgical tape.

3 Lie down. Place a smoky quartz on the front of each shoulder, and one on the floor touching the top of your head, all pointing away from the body.

4 Relax for 5–10 minutes, then remove the stones. Repeat daily for 4 days. If feelings persist, repeat for a further 4 days.

SELENITE MEDITATION

Certain ideas, emotions or memories can become "stuck" in your mind, arising unbidden, impossible to shake off, and triggering negative patterns of thought. This selenite crystal meditation quickly frees your aura from these unpleasant intrusions.

1 Select a long natural selenite crystal. Sit comfortably holding the stone between your hands so that the point or narrow end of the crystal is directed away from you.

2 Imagine a sphere of light suspended just in front of you, above your head. As you breathe in, imagine drawing light into the body with your breath. If you like, allow your mind to choose a colour or colours for the light.

3 Fill your body with this beautiful light. As you breathe out, imagine your breath focuses into the crystal and rapidly flows away from you, together with the feelings that you wish to release.

4 Continue this meditation until you feel clearer, and then take a few minutes just visualizing your breath flowing in and out through the selenite. This will infuse you with gentle cleansing energy and will help to seal your aura, preventing the return of the problem.

CHAPTER 4

COPING WITH CHANGE

In every period of history, in all areas of the world, mankind has attempted to explain, ease or avoid the experience of change. Eastern traditions tend to view change as part of the natural order – something we need to understand and harmonize with. Western religions tend to encourage us to surrender to the vicissitudes of life, and have faith in a better future or afterlife. But holding the belief that we can mould our destiny has been proven to contribute to our well-being. Crystal work puts the power to change our circumstances back into our own hands.

This chapter explores ways of using crystals to encourage stability and calm, ease fears and anxieties, and reduce mental confusion. We may not be able to alter a situation, but we can use crystals to help make changes within ourselves that reduce stress and minimize suffering.

MOONSTONE
(Potassium aluminium silicate)

KEYWORDS: Emotional balance, intuition
• *Stabilizes fluids in the body*
• *Releases tension*

SELENITE
(Calcium sulphate)

KEYWORDS: Expansion, acceleration
• *Soothes emotions*
• *Clears blocked energy*

A variety of the mineral feldspar, moonstone (or adularia) varies from greyish white to brown. Light reflecting off its internal surfaces creates opalescence and rainbow sparkles. It is usually found in microcrystalline form and large crystals are rare. In Sri Lanka (moonstone's main source) and India, it is the traditional Ayurvedic stone for women. Moonstone embodies the energy of the Goddess and the moon, linking it with fertility, growth, the cycle of time and the natural ebb and flow of energy. It works with the body's fluids and helps to release tensions that affect the functioning of the sacral and solar plexus chakras.

Selenite is a variety of the mineral gypsum. Formed by the evaporation of ancient seas, gypsum is the basis of plaster, cement, glass and paint. It has several other varieties, such as satin spar, desert rose and alabaster, which can vary from white or colourless to blue, yellow, brown or red. Selenite is colourless and can be recognized by its parallel grain. It is very soft and sensitive to water and humidity – it is easily scratched and will disintegrate and dissolve if left in water. One of the most powerful of the cleansing crystals, selenite shifts blocked or stagnant energy. Holding selenite can help to clarify thoughts and "move" negative emotions.

CLEAR QUARTZ
(Silicon dioxide)

KEYWORDS: Organizing, amplifying
- *Shifts energy*
- *Brings clarity*

RHODONITE
(Manganese silicate oxide)

KEYWORDS: Motivation, passion
- *Supports transformation*
- *Clears confusion*

Often known as "rock crystal", clear quartz contains no impurities and so appears completely colourless and transparent, though stones from different parts of the world differ in brightness and form. One of the world's most common crystals, it makes up more than a tenth of the Earth's crust. The stone has been used by shamans and healers for thousands of years to contact the spirit worlds, reveal the causes of illness and for divination. Clear quartz focuses thoughts and heightens perception, making it an ideal meditation aid. It also amplifies the energies of other stones and strengthens the aura, as well as cleansing and shifting energy.

Rhodonite is a silicate of manganese. Its colours range from pale pink to a deep rose red veined with black. Rhodonite's striking colour and mostly massive form make it an impressive ornamental stone. It is also used to produce ceramic glazes and pigments. Rhodonite aligns us to the underlying energy within creation and to our truest selves. This stone helps us to recognize deep truths, making it helpful during times of change, allowing us to find the best direction. It encourages the practical, positive expression of strong emotions. Sound activates rhodonite and causes it to resonate, so it is also a useful support for mantra meditation.

ROSE QUARTZ
(Silicon dioxide)

KEYWORDS: Love, emotion
- *Resolves issues of self-worth*
- *Releases deep-held feelings*

The characteristic pale pink of this stone is the result of minute amounts of titanium and manganese having been present during the formation of quartz crystals. It is usually translucent, with many fractures, and in microcrystalline, massive form. Transparent, gem-quality pale rose quartz is rare. Despite its gentle colour, this crystal has a strong, occasionally uncompromising effect. It works mainly on the heart chakra, releasing emotional stress and uncovering poor self-worth or intolerance, bringing issues to the surface to be cleared. Working with rose quartz for short periods will also balance and calm excess energy.

KUNZITE
(Lithium aluminium silicate)

KEYWORDS: Love, understanding
- *Resolves conflict*
- *Enhances self-esteem*

Kunzite is a variety of spodumene, coloured pink by manganese. The green variety is known as hiddenite. Kunzite crystals tend to be long, blade-like and striated. Its colour will seem more intense if viewed through its long axis. Used at the throat chakra, kunzite works to stimulate the whole body's energy levels. At the heart chakra it helps to improve self-esteem, quickly dissolving conflicts to leave clarity and tolerance. At the brow and crown chakras, this stone helps to create a secure, calm and clear mental space conducive to meditation. Kunzite also removes unhelpful energies from the aura, releasing negative thoughts and feelings.

RHODOCROSITE
(Manganese carbonate)

KEYWORDS: Self-confidence,
expansion
• *Relaxes muscles*
• *Releases tension*

Rhodocrosite has rose pink, pale
pink and cream concentric bands of
colour, and sometimes transparent,
deep rose pink rhombohedral crystals.
The gentle flow of these colours hints
at this stone's soothing properties.
It works on both the sacral and solar
plexus chakras, relaxing muscles
and releasing tension in the lower
abdomen to promote digestive flow
through the body. The stone gently
removes energy blockages, helping to
heal old emotional wounds that may
be impeding creativity or fertility.
Rhodocrosite is supportive and
calming, helping negative emotions
and judgments to fade away, leaving
the mind and emotions serene.

APOPHYLLITE
(Potassium calcium fluoro-silicate)

KEYWORDS: Nature, clarity
• *Cleanses energy channels*
• *Clears thoughts*

Apophyllite, a light, fairly soft crystal,
is often found in volcanic areas. Its
largest source is currently Poona,
India. Apophyllite's most common
form is a clear, four-sided pyramid
with sparkling, shiny surfaces. The
stone's brilliance reflects its ability to
lift emotions, lighten heavy memories
and resolve insecurities. It clears
thoughts and cleanses energy channels
gently but effectively. Working with
the green variety of apophyllite, which
has small, narrow crystals, helps
us forge closer links with Nature
and become more open to unseen
nature spirits. Both varieties provide
grounding with a light touch, useful
for channelling or clairvoyant work.

85

BIRTH AND NEW BEGINNINGS

Whenever we bring something new into the world – from the birth of a child to a new project at work – we call on the same qualities: vitality, nourishment, resourcefulness, focus and the ability to let go of old, unhelpful patterns of thinking or behaving. By supporting the chakras that govern these qualities, the crystal healing techniques on these pages encourage growth and help us to sustain new ventures.

All beginnings involve the energies of the root, sacral and solar plexus chakras, but the root chakra is the one that ensures the success and full manifestation of the birth process. It supplies the physical effort and the extra energy we require to give life to a new being or project. To support the continued life of this venture, we need sufficient resources to nourish and protect it: sustenance and resourcefulness are functions of the sacral and solar plexus chakras. The crystal net on the opposite page is useful for all types of beginnings, encouraging growth and self-protection while removing old habits and ensuring that the level of change feels comfortable.

CRYSTALS FOR NEW MOTHERS

In the weeks leading up to childbirth, a pregnant woman should surround herself with red crystals. The activating, sustaining energy they provide will help to nourish her own energy supplies – and she needs as much energy as possible to carry her through labour and delivery. Once the baby arrives, replace the red stones with orange and yellow crystals. The orange stones will help to dispel any shock and trauma, while the yellow stones will help to maintain nutrient and hormone levels. Yellow stones will also encourage a relaxed and cheerful atmosphere.

THE NET OF BEGINNINGS

In this net, a central axis of smoky quartz focuses and grounds personal energy, creating a quiet, protected space within which things can begin to grow. The complementary placements of rose quartz and celestite create a gentle polarity – warm is balanced with cool, active with passive, male with female – and this encourages creative potential to begin to manifest itself in concrete ways.

Smoky quartz × 3   Celestite × 3   Rose quartz × 3

1 Spread out a pale pink cloth on the floor and arrange the smoky quartz on it so that when you lie down they are positioned as follows: one below your feet on the midline of your body (pointing downward); one above your head (pointing toward you); and the third above it (pointing away from you).

2 Lie down in the net, aligning the midline of your body with the smoky quartz. Position the three celestite crystals on your right side (pointing away from you), level with your right hip, solar plexus and shoulder.

3 Place the three rose quartz at the same locations on the left side of your body, level with your left hip, solar plexus and shoulder.

4 Relax for 10–15 minutes before removing the stones. This net can be repeated daily if required.

DEATH AND ENDINGS

Endings are always with us. Some are welcome while others are difficult to cope with. They continually challenge our longing for certainty and security, and can instil a profound sense of failure or powerlessness. We tend to see ourselves, and to define our uniqueness, through the people, objects and routines we hold dearest. When these disappear, the image we have created of ourselves may start to disintegrate, only to be restored when we construct a totally new vision of our lives. Sometimes the loss can be so profound, however, that we lose our determination to redefine ourselves. Then the danger is that we will drift aimlessly, losing life-energy and deprived of hope or purpose.

Crystal healing can help to release the trauma of a loss. The crystal techniques set out here help to repair the body's subtle energy system while opening up new perspectives and broadening perceptions, in order to bring a sense of identity and the energy to start again.

THE MERLIN TECHNIQUE

This crystal layout will gently clear away unhelpful, negative attitudes and emotions, while encouraging creative solutions.

1 Select a black tourmaline, a blade-like kyanite crystal and a Herkimer diamond. Spread out an indigo-blue cloth and place the black tourmaline on top, so that when you lie down it will be below and between your feet.

2 Once you are lying down, tuck the kyanite crystal beneath your neck, close to the base of your skull and aligned with your spine.

3 Next, place the Herkimer diamond on the centre of your forehead.

4 Imagine you are breathing in indigo light for a moment or two, then relax. If tension, strong emotions or thoughts disturb you, resume the visualization.

5 Remain in the layout for 5–10 minutes before removing the stones. Repeat the technique every couple of days, when you feel it is necessary.

Nothing can remove the sorrow that accompanies a death, but it can be helpful to put your experience of grief in a broader context. Linking to star energy brings us a supra-mundane perspective, enlarging our experience of time and space, beginnings and endings, life and death.

Clear quartz × 7

1 Spread out a blue cloth on the floor and position the first quartz so that when you lie down it will be just above your head. Using three further crystals, make a diamond shape above the first quartz (with the points outward).

2 Place a fifth quartz on the midline of your body below where your feet will be, and make an equilateral triangle with the two remaining crystals, placing them below each foot, shoulder-width apart. Direct any points away from the centre of the triangle.

3 Lie down in the net for 10–15 minutes, then clear away the stones and relax for at least 20 minutes.

4 Repeat regularly until your enthusiasm for life returns. After a few sessions you may reduce your length of time in the net to 5–6 minutes.

THE SEVEN SISTERS

The Pleiades (or "Seven Sisters") are a faint cluster of stars linked to the return of life after the dark winter months in the Northern hemisphere. Myths surrounding this group of stars are similar worldwide, suggesting that the Pleiades were significant to mankind even before we began to disperse into Asia and the Americas 50,000–100,000 years ago. The myths link the stars with the end of suffering and the ability to cope at times of change, especially with grief. The stars symbolize hope and new starts and increase our awareness of nature's ever-renewing cycles.

89

STUDY AND EXAMS

Learning a new skill or studying calls on several different functions of the solar plexus chakra, which governs how we deal with information and the ways in which it is laid down in memory. Firstly, the information needs to be "filed" or labelled correctly so that it can be easily located when we need to retrieve it. Then we have to be able to interpret these memories accurately. Most people struggle with one or both of these steps, especially as we age and in situations of stress.

The techniques here harness the naturally orderly qualities of stone to support the solar plexus chakra and create a quiet, harmonious atmosphere conducive to efficient thought processes and memory skills.

AIR NET

Linked to the element air, this net of clear quartz ensures that information flows freely, making it ideal for times when our thoughts have become muddled or our focus blurred. It can also be useful for when you need to take a break from your studies but your mind continues to dwell on certain topics, or when you are unable to let go of worries about achievement or success.

1 Select six clear quartz crystals. Spread out a yellow cloth on the floor and position one of the crystals on top so that it is just above your head when you lie down (pointing upward).

2 Place a second crystal just below where your feet will be, in the midline of your body (pointing downward).

3 Place two crystals in line with your thighs, one on each side, pointing away from your body.

4 Place the last two crystals just beyond each shoulder, again pointing away from your body.

5 Lie down in the net for 3–5 minutes, then remove the stones. Repeat whenever you need to clear your thoughts.

This layout helps to stabilize the energy channels (meridians) associated with learning and information recall. The combination of yellow cloth and yellow crystals stimulates the solar plexus chakra. Choose stones that appeal to you.

Grounding stone
of your choice × 1

Yellow stone
of your choice × 2

Citrine
quartz × 2

1 Spread out a yellow cloth on the floor and position the grounding stone on top so that when you lie down it is below and between your feet.

2 Place the two yellow stones just below where each foot will be.

3 Lie down in the net and place the two citrines on the lower part of each side of your rib cage, about 2in (5cm) higher than your lowest rib. (Secure them with surgical tape if necessary.)

4 Relax with the stones in place for 4–6 minutes, then remove the stones. Repeat the net as frequently as required during periods of study, revision and examinations.

SUPPORTING STUDY AND MEMORY

To help with study, choose a large crystal as a learning or memory support. The best types are clear, rutilated or citrine quartz. Cleanse your chosen crystal thoroughly (see page 19), then sit with it for a few minutes and focus on your intention that the gem will support you in your learning and remembering. Keep the crystal close to you when you are studying or revising. Take it with you into exams as a "good luck" charm. If you become agitated or cannot remember something, gaze at the stone for a little while. When your studies are complete, cleanse the crystal again.

CHANGES IN LIFESTYLE

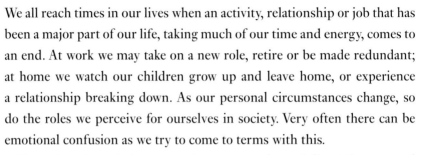

We all reach times in our lives when an activity, relationship or job that has been a major part of our life, taking much of our time and energy, comes to an end. At work we may take on a new role, retire or be made redundant; at home we watch our children grow up and leave home, or experience a relationship breaking down. As our personal circumstances change, so do the roles we perceive for ourselves in society. Very often there can be emotional confusion as we try to come to terms with this.

Crystal work can help us to gather our energies and direct them toward positive outcomes, even at times of profound change. The techniques shown here help us to come to terms with other people's changing expectations and to find the resources to adapt to new routines.

JUPITER NET

This net is linked to natural cycles of growth and expansion, represented by the planet Jupiter. It will help you to understand your place in the larger scheme of things and encourages a positive outlook and an openness to new possibilities.

1 Select twelve clear quartz crystals and spread out a dark blue cloth on the floor.

2 Place one quartz on the cloth so that when you lie down it will be below and between your feet. If the crystal is terminated, direct the point away from the centre of your body.

3 Place one crystal either side of the head, near to the shoulders, with any points directed outward.

4 Place four crystals on each side of your body, evenly spaced, with any points directed outward.

5 Lie down in the net and place the final crystal on the centre of your forehead, over your brow chakra, with the point directed upward.

6 Relax in the net for 4–8 minutes, then remove the stones. Repeat the net as often as required.

NEW PATHS LAYOUT

Try this layout to help you to deal with changes in your life, or when you need energy to tackle new challenges. Lapis lazuli brings clarity and insight, while the red cloth and stones activate a practical response to your change in circumstances.

Red stones of your choice × 2

Lapis lazuli × 1

Carnelian × 2

1 Spread out a red cloth on the floor. Position the two red stones of your choice on the front of each ankle (secured with surgical tape if necessary).

2 Lie down on the cloth and place a carnelian on your navel.

3 Place the lapis lazuli at the centre of your chest, over your heart chakra.

4 Place the second carnelian just below the lapis lazuli, at the base of your sternum. There is a small chakra here, the *anakananda*, which is associated with hopes and wishes.

5 Relax in the layout for 4–5 minutes, then remove the stones. Repeat daily until you feel your circumstances shift.

THE ENERGY OF NEW STARTS

Green tourmaline (also called verdelite) is one of the best stones to wear or use as a meditation aid to help us deal with a change of lifestyle. It helps to focus the body's subtle energy, balance emotions and free up thought processes, making it ideal for situations in which changes have taken place and new ways of being are emerging. The stone is especially useful when personal wishes have been overridden and the resulting emotions need to be resolved. Green tourmaline aligns us with universal energies, guiding us to find our own way and our independence.

MENOPAUSE

Menopause is not just the point in a woman's life when the body is no longer naturally fertile, it represents a time of substantial emotional and behavioural changes. These are caused by a reduction in the levels of the hormone oestrogen, triggered when the ovaries no longer have any eggs left to release and therefore cease to function. The body continues to make oestrogen, but at about 60 per cent of its previous level, and the liver and adrenal glands take time to adjust to this change. The symptoms accompanying this adjustment vary from person to person. Among the most common is the "hot flush", or sudden rise and then gradual fall in body temperature. The term "male menopause" refers to the emotional and behavioural changes that can occur in men between the ages of 45 and 60.

Crystal healing can help us to regain balance during this time of emotional and physical change. The techniques here help us to manage feelings of grief, heightened sensitivity and irritability while encouraging a new assertiveness and confidence.

PLUM TREE NET

The plum tree represents an energy pattern that supports self-empowerment and encourages practical solutions to problems. The combination of three crystals promotes the effective use of personal power and improves feelings of self-worth and motivation.

1   Select three crystals: one each of thulite, jet and jade. Spread out a pink cloth on the floor and position the piece of jet on top so that when you lie down it will be above your head.

2   Place the jade to the left of the jet, on a horizontal line with it and aligned with your left shoulder.

3   Place the thulite to the right of the jet on the same horizontal line and level with your right shoulder.

4   Lie down in the net for 5–6 minutes, then remove the stones. Repeat as required.

This layout supports the subtle-energy structures underlying the organs that help the body adapt to the hormonal changes of menopause. It also aids recovery from illness, especially colds and viruses.

Rhodonite
(tumbled) × 6

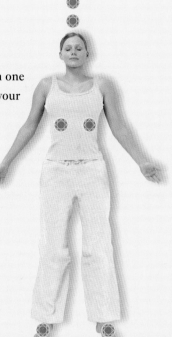

1 Spread out a yellow or green cloth on the floor. Position one rhodonite on top so that when you lie down it is above your head. Place a second stone directly above the first.

2 Place one rhodonite on each foot, on the tendons between your third and fourth toes. (Secure the gems with surgical tape if necessary.)

3 Lie down in the layout and place a stone on the lower part of each side of your rib cage, about 2in (5cm) higher than your lowest rib.

4 Remain in the net for 4–6 minutes, then remove the crystals. Repeat the layout whenever you feel the need.

THE THIRD STAGE OF LIFE

In spiritual terms, menopause represents the third stage in a woman's life as she completes her journey from maiden to mother to "crone" or wise-woman. In many cultures this is a time of celebration and of liberation from the constraints of domesticity. But in patriarchal societies, older women are often ignored or vilified, perhaps because they can be outspoken and openly challenge male dominance. Today drugs are often prescribed to delay the onset of menopause. However, the symptoms given as the reason for this intervention can also be eased through good nutrition, care to maximize immune function and protection from environmental toxicity, all of which can be supported by crystal healing techniques.

NEW ENVIRONMENTS

Most of us encounter new environments, such as a new workplace or home, at various points in our lives. These changes can be welcome, or a wrench away from the familiar; sometimes they can fill us with anxiety and trepidation. New environments, regardless of what they are, often trigger a range of similar concerns. They will often involve getting used to not only a new location, but also new people and new personal responsibilities.

In those who find new environments stressful it is often their own feelings that are the problem, rather than the situation. The techniques set out here therefore focus on acclimatizing the mind and emotions to an unfamiliar location. They are particularly appropriate for those who find the ambient energies of a new environment uncomfortable in some way, providing grounding and support. The key to these processes is always to adapt our own energy to accommodate the new circumstances we find ourselves in.

HARMONIZING BLACK TOURMALINE

Black tourmaline (also known as schorl) is an excellent crystal to help harmonize your personal energies with those of a new environment. Carry small black tourmaline crystals in your pockets or in a small pouch attached to your clothing. Alternatively, you can wear a black tourmaline as a pendant around your neck. In a new workplace, you can also tape a black tourmaline to the underside of your chair or desk, or keep one in a drawer. In a new house or other accommodation, place several black tourmaline crystals around the boundaries of the space, either inside or outside the walls. If you continue to feel unsettled, you can also place the tourmaline

in the same arrangement as the Earth Net (see page 39) on the floor – perhaps underneath your bed. While you are settling into the new environment, be sure to cleanse your crystals regularly (see page 19) to keep them working at maximum efficiency.

SETTLING VISUALIZATION

The combination of green and white stones used in this visualization will naturally harmonize your energy with unfamiliar surroundings.

1 Choose three green stones and three white or clear stones. Sit comfortably, in a chair or on the floor, or lie down, and place two white and two green stones around you – in any position that feels appropriate. Hold the remaining stones, one in each hand. Relax and let your body settle.

2 Take a few deep breaths in, feeling yourself become more relaxed with each out-breath. As you exhale imagine that your breath is moving into the crystals in your hands.

3 On your next out-breath, "send" the energy in the crystals in your hands into the stones placed around you. Repeat for five or six breaths.

4 Now imagine that the crystals around you are absorbing the energies of your environment. As you inhale imagine the energies from those stones moving into the ones in your hands. Then rest for a few breaths.

5 Take your attention to the crystals in your hands and imagine the energy in and around them slowly expanding until it fills your aura.

6 Allow the visualization to fade and return to everyday awareness. Cleanse your crystals thoroughly. Repeat the visualization as often as you like, until you feel more settled in your new space.

RELATIONSHIP PROBLEMS – PART I

Problems can arise in relationships when the interactive flow of energy and information between people is upset – in simplest terms this is an imbalance between giving and receiving. Many such problems are triggered by a behaviour trait that creates friction or irritation. This can lead to a change of mood or attitude in one person, which is then picked up by the other, causing the problem to escalate. The first step to resolve this is always to work with our own energy. Misunderstandings can be effectively reduced when we adjust our own stance and energy. Body language and subtle-energy signals in the aura reflect our emotional state and decision-making abilities long before our words confirm or attempt to disguise what we feel.

The techniques here work with our energies to help us alter our responses in difficult situations. This reduces friction and prevents the amplification of responses and aggravation of the original issue. Then, even if we cannot completely resolve an issue, we are likely to be less irritated by it.

RESOLVING CONFLICT LAYOUT

This layout helps to ease relationship problems. The iolite clarifies emotions and enhances compassion and understanding, while placing the stones at the heart and solar plexus chakras helps to bridge the divide between your feelings toward yourself and your feelings toward others. Placing a garnet at the feet boosts the whole energy system and makes you aware of the reality of the present moment.

1 Select one garnet and two iolite crystals. Place the garnet so that when you lie down it will be below and between your feet.

2 Lie down in the layout and place one iolite in the centre of your chest, over your heart chakra.

3 Place the second iolite midway between your navel and the base of your ribs, over your solar plexus chakra.

4 Remain in the layout for 3–5 minutes, then remove the stones. Repeat once a day until the situation eases.

BALANCING THE HEART LAYOUT

The heart chakra needs to be open if you are to experience the full range of your emotions – a closed heart chakra can lead to feelings of isolation or a lack of sensitivity to the feelings of others. However, if the chakra is too open, other people's emotions may seem overwhelming or you may feel disoriented. This layout helps to stabilize the emotions and open the heart chakra in a safe and protected way.

Grounding stone
of your choice × 1

Aventurine × 2

Clear quartz × 4

1 Place the grounding stone so that when you lie down it will be below and between your feet.

2 Lie down and place one aventurine on the centre of your chest, at your heart chakra.

3 Place four clear quartz points around the aventurine. Place one above it, pointing toward your throat; one below, pointing toward your feet; and one on either side, pointing away from the central crystal.

4 Place the second aventurine at the sternal notch at the base of your throat.

5 Remain in the layout for 4–5 minutes, then remove the stones. Repeat as required.

MAINTAINING YOUR BOUNDARIES

Labradorite can help you to deal with difficult issues within a relationship. This stone helps you to maintain your personal energy integrity – that is, it discourages you from overstepping other people's personal boundaries, and vice versa. This will give you more space within which to recognize both your own needs and those of others. Try wearing this gem as a pendant or carrying it in your pocket.

RELATIONSHIP PROBLEMS — PART II

"Three Views" is a simple pattern of three stones that aids the resolution of all sorts of problems and helps decision-making, and so it is ideal for working on interpersonal relationships. The technique is effective by itself or can be combined with meditation or visualization. It can help to clarify the mind and emotions when important choices need to be made, bringing fresh insight into possible courses of action. This technique is particularly effective in resolving tension between individuals.

THREE VIEWS: A MEDITATIVE HEALING

Trust your instinct as you move through this meditation. You will know without thinking which stones are appropriate and where to place them.

1 Gather all of your crystals together and spread them out so that you can see them all easily. Close your eyes and turn your thoughts to the situation with which you need help. Without analyzing or justifying your behaviour, become aware of how you have dealt with this situation up until now: for a moment simply observe how it has made you feel and how you have reacted.

2 Open your eyes and let them move over your crystals. One stone will attract your attention more than others – it may not be a stone you particularly like, just pay attention to where your eyes settle. This stone represents your personal energy in the current circumstances.

3 Repeat the process, this time closing your eyes and turning your attention to the other person. When you open your eyes, another crystal will attract your attention. This stone represents the relevant qualities of the other individual.

4 Close your eyes for a third time. Imagine a feeling of resolution within the conflict. Resist any impulse to intellectualize or plan, simply focus on your intention to reach a harmonious resolution. Open your eyes and select a third stone in the same intuitive manner as before. This stone represents the means of resolution.

5 Place the three stones in a clear space in front of you. You can arrange them in any way you like – experiment with some different arrangements.

6 Pick up the stone that represents you. Hold it in both hands. Where on your body do you feel that it needs to be placed or held? Put it there.

7 Take your attention to the stone representing the other person. Where does this belong in relation to the position of the stone representing you? It may be on your body as well, or more likely a little way away from you. Again, avoid intellectualizing, just put that stone where it feels "right".

8 Repeat the process for the stone representing the resolution of the issue. Again, place it on your body or somewhere near you.

9 With all the stones now placed, close your eyes and relax. Simply allow your awareness to expand until it encompasses the space you are in and the three crystals you have placed in relation to each other.

10 As you relax, the relationship of the crystals to each other and to yourself will begin to clarify and resolve the tensions within you that have prevented a positive solution. You may feel surges of emotion or inspiration as to how to proceed. After a few minutes take a few deep breaths and remove the stones. Cleanse them thoroughly. Repeat whenever you feel in need of help.

101

SERIOUS ILLNESS

Serious illness affects more than the physical body: it has a negative influence on every aspect of the subtle bodies, too – if not directly, then by depleting the amount of life-energy available to it. Whatever the symptoms and the prognosis, the body always benefits from as much deep rest as possible. Support this rest with crystal work, which also boosts the body's healing processes and helps to keep stress levels to a minimum.

SOURCE OF POWER NET

This net helps to restore vigour to the physical body. Carnelian supports your natural healing processes, while lapis lazuli stimulates the flow of energy and communication between all levels of the physical and subtle bodies.

1 Select a dark orange carnelian and three lapis lazuli. Spread out a violet cloth on the floor, lie down on it and place a lapis lazuli near the base of your spine (anywhere between the top of your calves to just below your coccyx).

2 Place the remaining two lapis lazuli on either side of your navel.

3 Place the carnelian in contact with the top of your head.

4 Relax for 3–4 minutes, then remove the lapis lazuli from your abdomen.

5 After a further 2 minutes, remove the other stones. Repeat regularly, until you feel strength returning.

This healing net allows us to access the finest and most profound of universal energies. It creates a stillness that removes mental distraction and physical hindrances, allowing the body maximum chance to restore itself.

Celestite × 1   Sodalite × 3   Turquoise × 3

1 Spread out a dark blue cloth on the floor (if you don't have a cloth this colour, visualize yourself inhaling indigo light for 3–4 minutes). Place the celestite on the floor at your earth star chakra; this is on the midline of your body at the same distance below your feet as the base of the spine is above them.

2 Place one sodalite crystal so that when you lie down it is on the midline of your body, between your calves.

3 Lie down and place the other two sodalites on the front of each hip bone, one on each side. (Keep them in place with surgical tape if necessary.)

4 Place the three turquoise gems on your upper chest: one on the thymus gland (half-way between the throat and heart chakras), and one close to each armpit.

5 Relax in the net for 5–10 minutes, then remove the crystals. Repeat every few days until you feel stronger, and then weekly for at least a month.

INTEGRATING PAST, PRESENT AND FUTURE

Use this technique when in the final stages of recovery from a long illness or deep shock, and at any time you need energy to make a new start. Spend a minute or two imagining that you are inhaling orange light (you can continue this visualization while the stones are in place if you wish). Place a haematite between your feet and a ruby outside each foot, at the same level. After 3–4 minutes remove the stones and hold a clear quartz crystal for the same length of time. Repeat as necessary.

SERIOUS ACCIDENTS

Even quite minor accidents can throw the body off-balance for some time. Serious accidents can completely change the way we approach life from that point on. In such situations we need to learn to adapt and to begin again. Not only does our body need to repair itself, we also have to adjust to becoming a different person, perhaps with new needs and capabilities.

Working with crystals offers a simple and non-invasive method to begin making repairs and readjustments right from the onset of recovery. Indeed, the faster the subtle bodies are returned to normal, the speedier any recuperation will be.

PERSIAN IRONWOOD NET

The energy of trees, with their inherent strength and flexibility, can be reassuring and comforting. Persian ironwood is a particularly resilient tree with many branches that grow into one another. It encourages deep stability and a sense of security and has been found to benefit those who have suffered in natural disasters, such as floods, storms and earthquakes. Similarly, in this net, amethyst quietens mental anguish and its placement reinforces personal control, "plugging" you back in to the planet's energy field. The background energy of the black cloth suggests the quiet, dependable and containing energy of the earth element.

1 Select six amethysts and spread out a black cloth on the floor. Place two stones so that when you lie down they will be below each foot, slightly out to the side.

2 Place one amethyst on the top arch of each foot. (Tape in place if necessary.)

3 Lie down and hold the last two amethysts, one in each hand.

4 Relax in the net for 4–5 minutes. Repeat several times a day if necessary, reducing frequency to once a day as your sense of security increases.

This net is effective at releasing the effects of old, deep-seated stress in the etheric body (see below) that cannot be resolved by other means. Carnelian and the colour orange are the quintessential remedies for shock, injury and emotional pain.

Carnelian × 6

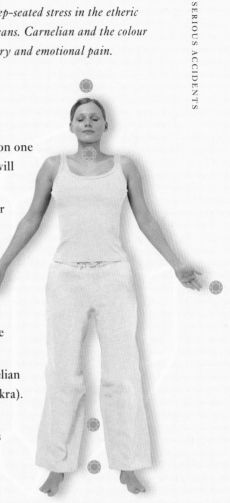

1 Spread out an orange cloth on the floor. Position one carnelian on top so that when you lie down it will be just above your head.

2 Place a second carnelian on the midline of your body, between your ankles.

3 Place another stone on the midline, this time between your calves.

4 Place a carnelian on either side of your torso, level with your sacral chakra (or your hip bones). You can place these stones either inside or outside your arms.

5 Lie down in the layout and place the last carnelian close to the base of your throat (the throat chakra).

6 Remain in the net for 6–10 minutes before removing the crystals. Repeat the technique as often as you require.

THE ETHERIC BODY

The etheric body is the layer of the subtle body closest to the physical body. It is the interface between our biological and spiritual selves, and so it can determine how quickly repairs are made to the physical body. Stress can easily get stuck in this layer, as it does in the sacral chakra. It is important to remove any such tension so that recovery can begin.

CHAPTER 5

FEEDING THE SPIRIT

Throughout history crystals have acted as magical items, playing a pre-eminent role in eliciting the help and reflecting the energy of the world of spirit. Most of the many different definitions of the word "spirit" point to one central idea: that it is an invisible but vital quality, without which any being loses its essential nature, its life-force. The levels of satisfaction and well-being that we sense in our lives can be significantly enhanced when we explore beyond the material confines of our everyday existence.

Crystals are an excellent non-denominational tool for broadening our perceptions, and the quietness and clarity that they create within us make them ideal for exploring meditative states. The layouts in this chapter help us to reveal different levels of awareness and access deep, intuitive knowledge often neglected in our present culture.

AMETHYST
(Silicon dioxide)

KEYWORDS: Integrating, calming
- *Enables all-round healing*
- *Maintains equilibrium*

OPAL
(Silicon dioxide with water)

KEYWORDS: Revealing, soothing
- *Encourages energy-flow*
- *Releases problems*

Amethyst's distinctive violet-purple colour is due to the presence of atoms of iron in its crystal lattice. Mostly found in igneous conditions, it usually forms as geodes – hollow rocks lined with crystals. It will turn yellow or brown if heated and fade if left in sunlight. Amethyst has been considered valuable for thousands of years, and in Classical Greece, the Middle Ages and the Renaissance was thought to encourage self-control and a spiritual outlook. It balances extremes of energy, making it a good all-round healing stone for any situation. It also calms emotions and over-active thoughts, so is a useful aid for meditation and sleep.

Opal is a type of quartz that has water lodged within its crystal lattice. When exposed to air, opal will release some of the water, which can leave the crystal fractured; placed in water, it will absorb more water molecules and expand; exposed to heat, it will release all of the water, removing the play of light characteristic of the crystal. Backing slivers of opal with other rocks or layering them does stabilize this gem, but it remains a brittle stone that needs care. In healing, opal has a soothing and releasing action, each stone's properties being focused through the chakra to which its colour corresponds (see page 25).

LABRADORITE
(Sodium calcium aluminium silicate)

KEYWORDS: Flexibility, protection
- *Increases body awareness*
- *Stimulates new ideas*

LAPIS LAZULI
(Sodium calcium aluminium sulphur silicate)

KEYWORDS: Truth, memory
- *Cleanses emotions*
- *Activates communication*

Labradorite is a variety of the mineral feldspar, found in igneous and metamorphic rock and distinguished by iridescent rainbow colours against a dark grey-green background. It helps to protect personal boundaries and energy, making it useful for a relationship that is draining, or that involves emotional manipulation. The stone increases our awareness of the body's physical and subtle limits, heightening our awareness of intrusions. This promotes a sense of security and safety, enhancing confidence and adaptability in encounters with others' emotions. Labradorite also helps us to access new ideas and opportunities.

Lapis lazuli contains blue lazurite crystals mixed with pyrite and calcite. High-grade lapis lazuli is a pure, rich mid-blue with flecks of golden pyrite. Lower-grade crystals include deposits of white calcite. This gem helps to bring clarity to any situation. If emotions or symptoms of stress are deeply held in, the release it causes can be powerful, but the peace that follows is welcome and restful. Closely linked to the brow chakra, lapis lazuli is an ideal meditation aid, bringing insight and stimulating intuition. Lapis also supports all types of communication and lends us the courage to speak the truth, especially in situations of injustice.

109

SODALITE
(Sodium aluminium chloro-silicate)

KEYWORDS: Meditation, peace
- *Stabilizes emotions*
- *Clears perception*

Sodalite can be easily confused with lapis lazuli (see page 109), but it is a deeper blue, never has pyrite inclusions (deposits) and is usually veined white. Sodalite works most effectively on thoughts and communication, supporting clarity of perception and intuition. The stone brings silence of thought which allows our consciousness to expand into other times, places and lives and there perceive subtle information. Sodalite can calm an over-active imagination and quieten the constant chatter of the everyday mind, bringing peace and contentment. This deep tranquillity helps the body to heal and recover after times of stress or illness.

FLUORITE
(Calcium fluoride)

KEYWORDS: Co-ordination, innovation
- *Structures thought processes*
- *Anchors ideas*

Found in a variety of colours, fluorite forms step-like crystals with cubic or rectangular sides. These visually striking single octahedral shapes occur naturally, but can also be cleaved from larger pieces. A fragile stone, fluorite needs to be handled carefully. It was the first mineral to be shown to fluoresce under ultra-violet light, and is the main source of fluorine gas and hydrofluoric acid. In healing, this stone creates order, and is useful for any task that requires careful planning or structuring. It helps to co-ordinate physical and mental abilities, and when used during periods of study, speeds up the learning process.

SAPPHIRE
(Aluminium oxide)

KEYWORDS: Precision, understanding
• *Regulates body systems*
• *Calms emotions*

Central and southwest Asia are the main sources of this stone; the finest pale blue sapphires are found in Kashmir. Usually coloured blue, sapphire can also be clear, yellow, green or orange. When this gem has rutile inclusions (deposits), it is often cut into domes to display the asterism (star-like shape) and called "star sapphire". In healing, sapphire supports the chemical messengers that affect the balance of bodily functions. It has a calming effect on the emotions, helping to reduce anxieties and tension. Used at the throat chakra, sapphire activates the ability to use subtle forms of communication and enhances self-expression.

PRESELI BLUESTONE
(Calcium aluminium silicate)

KEYWORDS: Grounding, timeless
• *Energizes head, shoulders and spine*
• *Protects and aligns*

Preseli bluestone is a form of dolerite found only in Pembrokeshire, Wales, UK. It formed deep within the Earth's crust more than 480 million years ago and was the material used to construct the inner rings of Stonehenge. The stone is either pure blue-grey or patterned with grey inclusions of feldspar. When polished, the stone becomes darker and the spotted variety resembles a starry night sky. This stone links us to the depths of the planet, helping us to feel connected to other times and places. Associated with the throat and brow chakras, it relaxes and energizes the head, shoulders and spine. Its healing effects can be amplified by the use of sound.

MOVING FORWARD

Moving forward in life requires a harmonious equilibrium between letting go of the old and welcoming the new, discarding the familiar and accepting the unknown and untried. Human beings seem predisposed to appreciate constancy and certainty, and to reject uncertainty and upheaval, even though the nature of existence is constant change. Moving forward often requires us to remodel our self-image to some extent, and thus many spiritual disciplines aim to break down the self-created boundaries that tie us to limited views of who we are, encouraging us to redefine our existence in a more integrated way.

The techniques set out here help us to address the characteristics we tend to cling on to – both positive and negative – that may be preventing us from breaking behaviour patterns, or recovering from illness or addiction.

GLASTONBURY THORN NET

Trees have to exist in harmony with their surroundings because, unlike people, they cannot run away or pretend that their circumstances are unchanging. The Glastonbury thorn is historically associated with a resting place reached after a long wandering, and, like all hawthorns, has close links with the heart chakra. Try this energy net if you feel that you need to clarify your direction in life and are in need of some rest to gain a better perspective.

1 Select twelve clear quartz and a ruby, and spread out a violet cloth on the floor. Arrange the quartz so that when you lie down one will be above your head and one on the midline of your body below your feet. Place five more evenly on each side of where your body will be. Direct the points outward.

2 Lie down in the net. Once you feel settled, place the ruby in the middle of your chest, over your heart chakra.

3 Relax for 5–10 minutes. Allow thoughts about your situation and your different options to float through your mind. New ideas may arise now, later or after several sessions. Remove the stones. Repeat as required.

SILVER BIRCH NET

The silver birch is traditionally associated with new beginnings, nurturing and illumination. This crystal net allows us to link to the qualities of this graceful tree. Trees, like crystals, have always been valued for their practical uses and symbolize endurance and stability as well as flexibility and adaptability. Combining the magical resonance of trees and stones in this net can powerfully realign your energies toward a new future.

Red granite × 1   Citrine × 1   Rose quartz × 2

1 Spread out a red or pink cloth on the floor (or visualize yourself inhaling red or pink light for 3–4 minutes). Lie down on the cloth and place the piece of red granite on the centre of your chest.

2 Place the citrine at the sternal notch at the base of your throat. If it has a point, direct the crystal downward, toward your feet.

3 Hold the pieces of rose quartz, one in each hand.

4 To enhance your connection with the silver birch, visualize your breath taking the following path: as you breathe in, imagine drawing air directly into your solar plexus. As you exhale, imagine the breath swirling around the inside of your body (like liquid swirling around a vessel).

5 After 5–6 minutes, remove the crystals and take some time to relax before returning to your daily routine. Repeat whenever you feel the need.

SHIFTING BLOCKS TO PROGRESS

Problems in our lives often arise when we cannot access the appropriate skills to deal with situations or are blocked by unhelpful patterns of behaviour. Crystal healing can help shift such obstacles by rebalancing the energy of the chakras to create optimum conditions for success.

These techniques work to reduce the effects of stress on the chakra system that are obstructing a desired outcome. The more direct the goals we work toward are, the easier our systems will adjust: it is better to state a specific intention such as "to pass my driving test", which will require a precise configuration of energies, than a general one such as "to improve my health", which may involve many different factors. These techniques need to be repeated regularly in order to bring about any real change.

FOCUSED CHAKRA BALANCE

Before you begin, define the goal that you wish to achieve, wording it as clearly as you can. Write the goal down on a piece of paper, to help to focus your attention and to keep as a record for future repetitions of the process. The more exact the message to your subtle bodies, the greater the likelihood of good results.

1 Sit comfortably and lay out your stones in front of you. Focus attention on the base of your spine, the site of your root chakra. Ask yourself, "Which crystal will balance my root chakra for this goal?" Be aware of the stone your eyes move to. Set it aside. It will balance and destress your root chakra.

2 Repeat for the remaining six chakras (see page 25). If your mind becomes too involved in the choice of gems, close your eyes and let your hands find the best one. Trust your intuition and your body. They understand the blocks in your way and can gauge the best crystal to resolve the situation.

3 When you have seven stones, select a grounding stone and place it by your feet. Lie down and place each stone on its chakra. Relax for 5–6 minutes. Remove and cleanse the stones. Wait at least a week before repeating the exercise for the same focus. It can be repeated for a different focus after four or five days.

This net uses the protecting, purifying qualities of white light, creating a clean slate and making way for new developments. The energy it releases can be quite strong, so be ready to bid farewell to redundant habits, objects or presences in your life.

Black tourmaline × 6

Clear quartz × 6

1 Spread out a white or black cloth on the floor. Place the black tourmalines so that when you lie down they will be as follows: one on each side of your torso level with your navel; one on either side of your legs at mid-calf level; and one on the midline of your body below your feet. Place the sixth tourmaline 10–12in (25–30cm) below this.

2 Place five of the clear quartz around where your upper body will be, one above your head, one beside each shoulder, and one on either side of your chest, level with your heart.

3 Place the last quartz crystal either below the tourmalines, to emphasize purification and cleansing, or 10–12in (25–30cm) above the quartz at the crown of your head, to encourage new potential.

4 Lie in the net for 5–10 minutes, then remove the stones. This can be repeated weekly if required.

BALANCED POLARITIES

Whether you choose a white cloth or a black cloth in this net, the same effects are achieved, but by different means. White signifies clarity, purity and the emptiness of all potential, while black represents silence and pre-existence and the emptiness of all manifestation. Black and clear stones work in similar ways: clear quartz emphasizes space and clarity; tourmaline the potential and basis for future action. Black without white would remain dormant, and white without black would leave potential undefined.

REMOVING NEGATIVE PATTERNS

When it comes to our individual well-being, any influence that shifts our energy system out of equilibrium we will experience as negative. The stressors in themselves may not be "bad" or harmful, but any loss of balance, particularly if it cannot be immediately compensated for, sets up repercussions that travel through all levels of the body, upsetting the smooth working of the whole. Despite this, nearly all of us "get by" in a state of false equilibrium in all levels of the self: physical, emotional, mental and spiritual. This working balance is maintained by constantly compensating for energetic blocks, stresses and imbalances – essentially, we work around our problem areas.

Our bodies can function adequately in this way during the quiet periods of life, but all the time we restrain these disruptive influences, large amounts of our life-energy are siphoned off, restricting our flexibility and adaptability. We feel the lack of readily available energy especially strongly when stress factors increase. Then, the added pressure on the system weakens the functioning of the body at every level, and symptoms of physical infection, emotional and mental turbulence, and spiritual distress begin to appear.

The more stress that is placed on our system, the greater our tendency to respond to circumstances and stimuli in a negative way. Theoretically, if an individual were completely stress-free and in perfect equilibrium, no experience would have a negative impact on them because their infinite adaptability could accommodate and integrate all situations.

Any healing technique that helps to release and eliminate the effects of stress, whatever its origin, will, therefore, also remove patterns of negativity. The Figure of Eight Layout on the opposite page is just such a technique. It helps to clear our systems of stress and energy blocks, helping us to adapt to new circumstances and stressors instead of allowing a build-up of negative experiences.

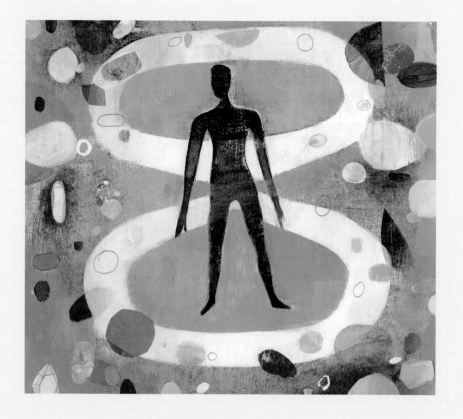

FIGURE OF EIGHT LAYOUT

This procedure derives from a kinesiology technique, itself derived from Tibetan sources that identify a number of energy loops in the body. In this version, a figure-of-eight pattern encloses the body, creating a dynamic sweep of energy through and around it. This dislodges inappropriate energy, activates natural healing processes, and "ties together" energies torn apart by trauma or illness. It can be used whenever you detect sluggishness or inactivity in your body, mind or emotions. These crystals are grounding and protecting, and will powerfully neutralize stress and negativity.

1 Select eleven crystals, either all smoky quartz or all black tourmaline.

2 Arrange ten stones so that when you lie down there is one below your feet, two on each side of your legs, two on each side of your torso, and one above your head. Place them asymmetrically to encourage a dynamic energy flow.

3 Lie down and place the last stone on your abdomen to complete the figure of eight. Relax here for up to 10 minutes, then remove the stones. Repeat daily during stressful times.

117

COSMIC STRESS

Cosmic stress is caused by those influences that sweep across Earth as a result of the ever-changing relationship between the sun, moon and planets. We are innately and biologically programmed to react to cosmic events such as sunrise and sunset, the changing of the seasons and lunar cycles. But occasionally we also become sensitive to less obvious planetary happenings. There is plenty of evidence to suggest that plant and animal life cycles are sensitive to lesser-known cosmic events, such as the movements of Venus, Mars and Jupiter. It follows that the same applies to human beings. Modern lifestyles may mask these subtle influences on us, but when we feel particularly vulnerable or notice that "something is not quite right", cosmic stress may be at work – disturbed sleep cycles and mood variations, for example, are often related to phases of the moon.

Crystals can ease the effects, as in the net opposite. Indian Ayurvedic medicine has always used crystals in remedies for astrological stress, using the unique planetary positions in an individual's birth chart to prescribe healing gems. When choosing your own stones for this purpose, allow your deep instincts to draw you to the most helpful crystal.

COPPER HEALING

Copper has been associated with Venus, the planet also known as the morning and evening star, for thousands of years (see page 59). This mineral's conductivity and flexibility have made it invaluable in electrical technologies, properties which have no doubt influenced its use in popular folk medicine as a way of reducing inflammation and pain from arthritis and rheumatism. It can also be used to alleviate cosmic stress. If you feel a sense of heaviness, confusion or clumsiness and suspect it may be because of astrological or other seasonal and planetary effects, wearing some copper for a day will verify this. If your symptoms lessen, then they are cosmic in origin. If they persist, the problem lies elsewhere.

The dark pink cloth used in this net helps to focus healing into your subtle bodies, where the effects of cosmic events are registered. Combined with the grounding properties of tourmaline, dark pink creates a calming, unifying energy that reduces aggravation and irritability, integrating your whole body with the energy of the planet.

Black tourmaline × 1   Green tourmaline × 2   Blue tourmaline × 1   Pink tourmaline × 1

1   Spread out a dark pink cloth on the floor. If you can, align the cloth so that when you lie down, your head is in the most northerly direction. (If you don't have a cloth this colour, visualize yourself inhaling dark pink light for 3–4 minutes.)

2   Position the black tourmaline so that when you lie down it is on the midline of your body, below your feet.

3   Place the green tourmalines on either side of your body, level with your heart.

4   Place the blue tourmaline above where your head will be when you lie down. Position the pink tourmaline above it.

5   Lie down and check that your body is correctly aligned within the net, and that the stones are in the correct positions.

6   If you are not using a cloth, visualize your body and the crystals being surrounded by and supported within a cocoon of dark pink.

7   Relax for 5–10 minutes, then move out of the net and cleanse the stones thoroughly (see page 19).

8   Take plenty of time to recover from this net before resuming normal activities. Repeat every couple of days or more frequently, until you feel more like your usual self.

INITIATION CYCLES

All of us encounter challenges that bring about change in our lives. There are actually four specific times in most people's adult lives that present particular opportunities to change and evolve. These cycles of personal development are based on the time that the outer planets of the solar system take to journey around the sun. Depending on the individual, the challenges and changes may occur in different spheres of life – from family to career – but still share underlying themes, set out in the chart below. Understanding that these circumstances have arisen because we have reached a certain age can put them into context, remove fear and help us take positive steps to adjust and move forward. Crystal healing can help us to integrate change into our lives and give us the confidence to tackle challenges head on.

CYCLES OF TRANSFORMATION

AGE	CHALLENGES	HELPFUL CRYSTALS	HELPFUL NETS
28–32	• To reflect on what you have achieved • To let go of patterns of behaviour learned from your family • To become an individual in your own right	Green tourmaline (page 150), turquoise (page 132)	Saturn Net (page 69); Earth Net (page 39)
39–42	• To begin to embrace a more spiritual view of the world • To break away from limiting social ties • To recognize that patience is essential • To cope with radical change	Smoky quartz (page 34), amethyst (page 108), rhodonite (page 83), tiger's eye (page 147)	Pluto Net (page 66); Neptune Net (page 78); Uranus Net (page 121)
49–51	• To heal yourself physically • To deal with issues from childhood that still hold you back • To take a leap of faith into a future you yourself have determined	Turquoise (page 132), Preseli bluestone (page 111), lapis lazuli (page 109)	Chiron Net (page 55); Unconditional Being Net (page 71); Etheric Body Net (page 105)
58–62	• To let yourself become who you really are • To take steps toward a new beginning • To understand fully that the only person who limits you is yourself	Rubellite (page 153), tourmaline (page 34), danburite (page 154)	Jupiter Net (page 92); Saturn Net (page 69)

This net links your energies to those of the planet Uranus, associated astrologically with the drive to break away from old patterns and a need to be different. These energies increase intuition and encourage creative and innovative behaviour. When you experience difficulty or disruption in your life, use this net for empowerment. It is particularly effective when you are feeling oppressed or trapped.

Green stones of your choice × 6

Clear quartz clusters × 6

1   Spread out a pink cloth on the floor. (If you don't have a cloth this colour, visualize yourself inhaling pink light for 3–4 minutes.) Place the green stones of your choice on the floor so that when you lie down they are as follows: one above your head; one below your feet; one on either side of your thighs; one on either side of your shoulders.

2   Lie down within the net, and place the clear quartz clusters on your body as follows: one on the centre of your pubic bone; one just inside each hip bone (secured with surgical tape if necessary); one in each of the hollows between your armpit and collarbone; and one on the centre of your forehead.

3   Relax in the net for 4–6 minutes. If you are not using a cloth, repeat the pink light visualization. Then remove the clear quartz clusters and place them a short distance away from your body.

4   Remain within the green stones for a further 2–3 minutes before getting up from the net. Cleanse your crystals thoroughly. Repeat regularly: every 3–4 days, or as required.

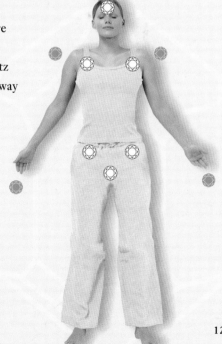

PAST AND OTHER LIVES

The concepts of past lives and reincarnation are well-established in many spiritual traditions, and our desire to access these previous experiences has generated many forms of past-life healing. Although such practices are potentially useful for releasing stresses, there are also risks, including becoming too identified with past life experiences. The value of past-life work lies in its ability to help us recognize behavioural traits that repeat themselves and prevent us from letting go of damaging habits. If these tendencies can be removed, the energy they use up can be reintegrated into the body, bringing the possibility of very deep healing.

There are many methods for achieving this reintegration – most of them derived from shamanic traditions of soul retrieval and work with ancestor spirits. Any form of healing that ventures into deep levels of the unconscious mind must be handled with extreme caution. The techniques offered here focus only on issues that our bodies will be willing and able to deal with, while establishing a safe, supportive environment for healing.

DEEP MEMORY LAYOUT

This layout can help you to recall memories from many years ago – or even from other lives. It uses amazonite to help you understand and locate links to the past. Don't worry if you are unable to grasp the information it provides in a conscious way immediately. Your body will access the knowledge it needs, but it may take a few days to filter into your conscious mind.

1 Select two amazonite crystals. Place one on the back of your neck at the base of the skull (securing it with some surgical tape if necessary).

2 Lie down and place the second crystal at the centre of your chest, over your heart chakra.

3 Relax for 4–6 minutes, then remove the stones and cleanse them. Leave at least 4 days between repeat sessions.

This was the first net we developed, back in the early 1980s. It is a general net for retrieving and integrating fragmented parts of the self, and can be used for safe regressions, deep healing work and clarifying all levels of personal energy.

Amethyst × 8

1 Spread out a yellow or violet cloth on the floor (or visualize yourself inhaling yellow or violet light for 3–4 minutes).

2 Arrange the stones on top so that when you lie down they will be as follows: one on the midline of your body below your feet; one outside each leg at knee-to-calf level; one on each side of your waist (outside your arms); one on each side of your shoulders; and one above your head. If the stones are different sizes, place the largest by your feet, and form equal-size pairs. Direct any points toward the body, or use tumbled stones.

3 Focus on the intention to heal any issues from other lives that it is appropriate to tackle. If you are not using a cloth, repeat the light visualization.

4 Lie in the net for at least 5–10 minutes before getting up. Repeat as often as required.

OTHER USES FOR THE AMETHYST NET

The amethyst net brings a quiet calm to any agitated states of body and mind. If you are unsure how to approach a particular health concern with crystals, it is always a good place to start. You can also use the net to explore the properties of other crystals. After a few minutes in the net, place a different crystal on your forehead and observe its effect.

MEDITATION WITH CRYSTALS

In modern society, taking a break from activity is often perceived as wasting time. This is an incorrect perception that can lead us to underestimate the nature of meditation and what it can do for us. There are many different methods for attaining a meditative state, but at its most fundamental, meditation simply means focusing attention on a particular aspect of life. The potential benefits are clear-sightedness, inner stability, relaxation and better orientation toward goals.

If you have already tried out some of the crystal healing layouts in this book, you will be familiar with the feel of a meditative state – it occurs naturally during crystal healing work. As the crystal and human energy fields interact, we feel a deep relaxation, the body quietens and the mind experiences inner focus, though we remain aware of our surroundings. Much crystal work is carried out lying down, so there is a tendency to drift into a near-sleep state. However, you can achieve the same deep level of relaxation and mental clarity while seated comfortably, and sitting can make it easier to be aware of changing levels of perception.

If you have a couple of favourite crystal nets, you may like to begin crystal meditation by spending a few minutes lying in one of them – this acclimatizes your body to a state of deep relaxation and can make the gazing technique on the opposite page easier to accomplish.

CRYSTAL GAZING

For this exercise you will need a large clear quartz crystal. Other stones can be used, but transparent crystals work best, especially for beginners. A cut and shaped sphere is ideal, or a good-sized natural crystal with one large facet that allows you to look into the stone.

1 Sit in a comfortable position in which you can keep your spine straight. Place your chosen meditation crystal in front of you. If it needs support, place it in a container of sand or pebbles. Take a few deep breaths in and out and relax your face and eyes. Allow your eyes to find a comfortable angle from which to view the crystal: a slightly downward gaze is usually ideal.

2 Let your eyes take in the crystal, but do not focus them. Just gaze in a relaxed manner. When you find you are focusing on a particular area of the crystal, simply relax your eyes again. As you continue to gaze in a relaxed way, allow the sight of the crystal and its surroundings to flow effortlessly into your eyes, without letting your mind comment or pass judgment.

3 While you continue to sit and gaze, keep your whole body relaxed and allow your other senses to be passive. Let sounds and sensation come and go and thoughts arrive and depart: you do not need to pay attention to them.

4 When your awareness wanders, take your attention to your breath moving in and out. Open your mouth slightly and notice the cool air passing over your palate as you breathe in. As you exhale, notice that you don't feel the warm air passing over your palate. Maintain awareness of this experience.

5 Continue your crystal-gazing meditation for 5–10 minutes, then relax. Repeat as often as you like.

DEALING WITH DISTRACTION

Using crystals in meditation encourages the body and mind to quieten. Clear crystals have a cooling, clarifying effect when you gaze into them, and have a natural fascination for the mind, making it less likely to wander away on thought-stories. But when you do, inevitably, find yourself in the middle of a daydream, simply return your attention to the image of the crystal and let it fill your eyes. Do not try to stop, or escape, from your thoughts – instead, simply turn your attention away from them.

AIDS TO MEDITATION

Because of their inherently stable structure, crystals can be powerful aids to meditation practice. Stones of any type can act as a focus for the mind and senses, allowing the crystalline properties of coherence and stillness to quieten the mind's superficial activity and permit more profound and elemental patterns of energy to emerge into awareness.

The qualities that crystals are known to exhibit have been linked to the constant flow of free electrons within their lattice structure. It is likely that we interact with these fields of energy via our own electromagnetic fields, especially the powerful ones of the brain and heart: the pulsating patterns created by brainwaves, heartbeats and sound sources set up resonant feedback loops between humans and crystals at the fundamental level of the electron. Crystals may even store these vibrations in some way, releasing them when an appropriate stimulus is applied. This raises the prospect that crystals store or amplify many types of wave, including sound and thought vibrations. Thus, a crystal you use within the context of meditation on one occasion may reinforce successive practices with positive feedback loops between the crystal lattice and your own neural net.

CONTEMPLATIVE QUARTZ

Quartz is particularly useful for meditation. All types of quartz encourage a bright, clear quietness that calms the physical body but keeps the mind alert. Holding a clear quartz in your right hand and a smoky quartz in your left creates a dynamic polarity that quietens your body's energy levels and enhances sensory awareness. Use stones that are large enough to hold comfortably. Both natural and tumbled stones are suitable for meditation.

WORKING WITH YOUR CRYSTALS

The best way to start meditating with crystals is to sit with them or practise the gazing exercise on page 125. Enjoy simply existing, with no purpose and without reasoning or passing judgment. These tips address common concerns for beginners.

- Avoid the idea that physical, mental or emotional stillness is required for meditation. All you need to do is prevent yourself from being absorbed by any thoughts, sensations or outside experiences.

- Relax into restlessness: trying to suppress energy stirs up more energy. Just allow all thoughts and sensations to come and go in their own time.

- If one part of your body starts to ache or feels stiff, take your attention to that area. If you are holding a crystal and can reach that part of the body, move the crystal there too. Keep your attention and the crystal in that part of the body for a few minutes and then return to your meditation.

- If a ticking clock, another person's breathing or traffic noise disturbs you, focus on that sound. For a few minutes, allow your mind to explore it thoroughly, before returning to your meditation.

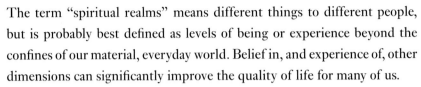

SPIRITUAL REALMS

The term "spiritual realms" means different things to different people, but is probably best defined as levels of being or experience beyond the confines of our material, everyday world. Belief in, and experience of, other dimensions can significantly improve the quality of life for many of us.

Crystals are excellent tools for broadening our perception and experience of the finer levels of existence. As with any exploration of subtle energy, it is important to ground your energies after this kind of work. We suggest, therefore, that after using the techniques on these pages, you use a grounding layout such as the Earth Net (see page 39), or sit and hold a grounding stone like black tourmaline or smoky quartz.

ETHER NET

In the Indian Vedic tradition the element ether (akasha) is the container that holds the four other elements – fire, earth, air and water. This net focuses your awareness on underlying stillness, helping you to move away from everyday patterns into a refreshing, open space. Celestite is a heavy, pale blue crystal that lifts the emotions and clarifies thoughts.

1 Select seven small clusters, points or tumbled celestite, two grounding stones of your choice and spread out a white cloth on the floor. (If you don't have a white cloth, visualize yourself inhaling white light for 3–4 minutes.) Place the grounding stones within easy reach.

2 Arrange the celestite stones on the cloth so that when you lie down they are positioned as follows: one beside each foot; two on either side of your body, spaced evenly apart; and one above your head.

3 Lie down in the net for 4–5 minutes.

4 Remove the celestite stones and place one grounding stone beneath your feet and a second at the base of your throat. Relax with these in place for 3–4 minutes, then remove the stones. Repeat as required.

FEEDING THE SPIRIT

By setting a clear intention before you begin, you can use this net to access specific dimensions or spiritual realms. It can also be used more generally to deepen your inner communication, explore finer levels of the self or reinforce your subtle energy boundaries. Although we should not be separated from any part of ourselves, we still need firm boundaries to prevent unwelcome intrusions from outside energies.

1 Choose intuitively from your collection three sets of five crystals of the same type (fifteen crystals in all). Intuitively decide which set will be positioned in line with your brow chakra, heart chakra and root chakra.

2 Place four of the brow-line crystals so that when you lie down there are two on each side of your head, in a line extending in a wide V-shape upward from the top of your head.

3 Place two of the heart-line crystals on each side of your body, in a line extending horizontally away from your torso, level with your heart chakra.

4 Place two of the root-line crystals on each side of your legs, extending in an wide upside-down V-shape toward your feet from the level of the hip bones.

5 Lie down between the crystals and place the remaining root-line crystal near the base of your spine; the remaining heart-line crystal over the heart chakra at the centre of your chest; and the remaining brow-line crystal at the centre of your forehead.

6 When all the crystals are in place, briefly send your awareness out to each of them and then relax.

7 Remain in the layout for 5–10 minutes. Remove the stones and rest for a further 15 minutes before returning to normal activities. Leave at least a week between repeat sessions.

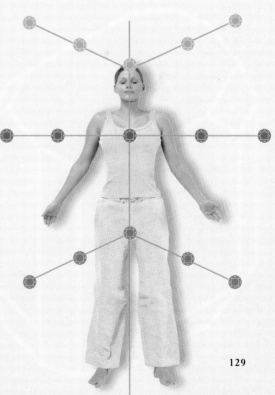

CHAPTER 6

LIVING IN HARMONY

We live in an imperfect world. No matter how skilled we are at maintaining the health of our bodies and balancing our emotions and mental processes, we cannot eliminate the influence of our surroundings. We are exchanging matter all the time, in the air we breathe and in the food and drink we consume and eliminate. We constantly renew our cellular material: every atom in our bodies is replaced within a few years.

We are what we eat, but we are also where we live, though few of us can choose precisely where we work or make our homes in order to avoid environmental problems. What we can do is make adjustments within ourselves to reduce unavoidable stresses. This chapter explores the ways crystals can protect us from issues like electromagnetic stress and harmonize our energies with those of our surroundings.

TURQUOISE
(Copper aluminium phosphate)

KEYWORDS: Strength, protection
- *Harmonizes energy*
- *Balances all systems of the body*

Turquoise is a copper mineral found mostly in desert regions. Its colour varies from blue to green – a stone's exact shade can be used to identify the mine it came from. Turquoise is delicate and is often treated with wax or resin to stabilize its colour and form. This is an all-purpose healing stone that protects the whole being (physical and subtle) by repelling negative energy, but it is particularly effective when used on the heart, thymus and throat. Turquoise calms emotions and brings harmony to discordant thoughts. It can also be used to enhance psychic skills and connections to spirit worlds.

AVENTURINE
(Silicon dioxide)

KEYWORDS: Balance, stability
- *Encourages a positive outlook*
- *Increases tranquillity*

A microcrystalline quartz with sparkly flecks, aventurine is thought of as the "good luck" stone because it shares a name with aventurine glass (from the Italian *avventura*, "by chance or fortune"). The man-made glass, created by accident in 17th-century Venice, Italy, has similar flecks. Aventurine has been widely used for jewelry, ornaments and carvings since antiquity. In healing, all aventurines help the body to relax and increase feelings of contentment. Green aventurine, the most common type, works with the heart chakra to balance and stabilize emotions. The stability it provides leads to clearer, calmer thoughts.

BLOODSTONE
(Silicon dioxide)

KEYWORDS: Courage, support
- *Motivates new endeavours*
- *Improves strength and health*

Also known as heliotrope, bloodstone is a type of chalcedony quartz. Its green colour is caused by actinolite or mica and the red markings by iron oxides. Good-quality bloodstone has distinct red marks, while lower grades have larger areas of grey. In crystal healing, the stone creates a balance between the heart and the root chakras. This helps to boost physical strength and maintain emotional well-being, encouraging new drive and enthusiasm. Traditionally worn for protection against injury and loss of blood, this gemstone protects the life-force. It also encourages the practical use of subtle skills such as psychic perception.

JADE
(Jadeite: sodium aluminium silicate) &
(Nephrite: calcium magnesium ferro-silicate)

KEYWORDS: Belonging, instinct
- *Stimulates healing processes*
- *Confers stability*

Two related minerals with similar properties are given the name "jade". Jadeite (a pyroxene) is less common than nephrite (an actinolite), but is found in a wider range of colours. The depth of green makes good-quality nephrite easy to identify, whereas a lower-quality might be confused with jadeite. In healing, jade is used to enhance kidney function and stimulate kidney *chi* energy, which is associated with long life and the maintenance and support of all the body's healing processes. Jade encourages a sense of tradition and of relationship to one's ancestors, which nurtures feelings of security, belonging and deep stability.

BLUE LACE AGATE
(Silicon dioxide)

KEYWORDS: Comforting,
gently cooling
• *Instils peace*
• *Nurtures body and mind*

AQUAMARINE
(Beryllium aluminium silicate)

KEYWORDS: Cooling, clarifying
• *Activates positive energy*
• *Stimulates flow of ideas*

Blue lace agate is a variety of chalcedony quartz with bands of violet, blue and grey. It is generally available as tumbled stones or slices, but also sometimes as geodes (hollow rocks lined with crystal). Namibia in southwest Africa is a major source. The pale, gentle colours of blue lace agate are deeply soothing, bringing calm and peace to every level of being. This pacifying effect helps to disperse built-up energy, encouraging relaxation and a sense of respite from immediate problems. Healing with blue lace agate mitigates emotional hurt and alienation, and encourages a willingness to explore the world and welcome new experiences.

This is the blue variety of the beryl family of stones. Fine aquamarines are often used in jewelry, but non-gem-quality tumbled stones are widely available for use in healing. Aquamarine has sides clearly striated into parallel lines, an indication that the stone moves energy quickly, dissolving blocks and barriers. The stone works with the immune system to strengthen the body's defences. Aquamarine clears negative emotions, replacing them with optimism. It directs inspiration toward practical goals and empowers those who lack courage or self-belief. Traditionally, it was worn as a protective talisman for journeys, especially by sea.

AMAZONITE
(Potassium aluminium silicate)

KEYWORDS: Stimulating, releasing
- *Facilitates personal expression*
- *Encourages communication*

MALACHITE/AZURITE
(Copper carbonate)

KEYWORDS: Protecting, transmuting
- *Relieves pain*
- *Expands potential*

A variety of feldspar, amazonite is usually pale turquoise to mid-green interspersed with narrow streaks of white. High-quality amazonite crystals are a clean turquoise blue with less visible areas of white. Amazonite is fairly soft and easily worked, so it has a long history of use for jewelry and ornaments. The stone is associated with protection and with our links to people and events in the past, and it can be used to improve memory and psychic skills. Amazonite works particularly well at the throat chakra to release blocked emotions, and to support communication where there are difficulties.

The copper compounds malachite and azurite are often found together – when azurite oxidizes, it becomes malachite. Azurite is a rich deep blue. Malachite is deep green with concentric bands of darker green or black. Both are soft minerals and have been carved into beads and ornaments for thousands of years. Malachite eases physical pain and aids recuperation after exhaustion. It is a protective stone, and especially helps the body cope with environmental pollutants. Both azurite and malachite bring underlying stresses to the surface to be released. This frees up energy that can then be used to develop personal potential.

135

ELECTROMAGNETIC STRESS

We are surrounded by electrical devices at home, at work and in the car – we even carry them with us. Each one generates an electrical field, which influences our surroundings. Since our bodies are composed largely of water, an excellent electrical conductor, and our internal systems rely on minute electrical currents, we cannot avoid being continually affected. All living beings have their own electromagnetic field (EMF), generated by the chemical and cellular activity of the body. When surrounded by other strong EMFs, that field becomes "entrained", taking on some of the characteristics of the larger field.

As our body strives to maintain its focus, we may start to feel drained and to experience constant tiredness. Other symptoms of an upset electrical balance include problems with immunity, loss of concentration, mood changes, insomnia, dizziness, eye problems, joint pain, agitation, and sensitivities to food or chemicals. The crystal healing techniques on these pages offer ways to insulate yourself from the deleterious effects of electromagnetic stress.

PLACEMENTS FOR PROTECTION

Placing crystals close to electrical appliances can help to counteract their EMFs, but the stones need to be cleansed daily to remain effective. Carrying or wearing smaller crystals is a good way to protect yourself wherever you go. The following placements are particularly effective:
- Around the neck, to protect the throat.
- On the thymus gland, between the centre of the chest and the throat.
- On the centre of the chest (the site of the heart chakra).
- In the lap when seated.
- On the floor between the feet.

   Particularly useful crystals include: black tourmaline, labradorite, Preseli bluestone, turquoise, malachite, chrysocolla.

DEALING WITH ENTRAINMENT

Use this technique after spending time in an environment filled with computers, or after a long journey by car, rail or air. It is also effective when you have difficulty detaching yourself from the day's experiences. The movement of the iron-rich, magnetic stone helps to break up entrainments and restore the natural patterns of your personal energy field.

Lodestone × 1

1 Select a small piece of lodestone or magnetite (the latter is more widely available). Place it in a metal spiral and then tie a thread securely to the spiral to create a pendulum. Keep the thread relatively short, so it can swing rapidly and stay under your control.

2 The procedure can be carried out lying down, seated in a chair or standing, although you may find the latter easiest if you are practising this on yourself.

3 Take a firm grip on the thread. Start the pendulum spinning, then move it steadily through your own or the other person's aura, about 6–8in (15–20cm) from the body.

4 Working systematically, cover as much of the body as possible, front and back, including the soles of the feet. Take as long as you need to complete the exercise. This can be repeated daily if required.

137

GEOPATHIC STRESS

Geobiology is the study of the relationship between the Earth and all forms of life; geopathic stress is the energy generated by the Earth that causes problems for those life forms. Many forces occur naturally within and around our planet, such as air and ocean currents. The field of energy surrounding us expands as the Earth spins from sunrise to noon, and then contracts from noon to sunset. It also changes according to the lunar cycle and is affected by other cosmic events, such as the movement of other planets, meteor showers and the orbit of comets.

There are two important regular energy patterns, named the Hartmann Net and the Curry Grid after the scientists who discovered them. We might think of them as vertical screens of energy, and they are often depicted as networks crisscrossing the surface of the planet. Both patterns take the form of regular "standing" waves that can be detected, with a little practice, by dowsing and sensing.

The lines of the Hartmann Net are 2–10in (5–25cm) wide, and run from north to south and east to west, around 6.5ft (2m) apart. The lines of the Curry Grid can be up to 20in (50cm) wide, and run from north-west to south-east and south-west to north-east, some 9–26ft (3–8m) apart. The width of the lines varies according to the cycles of the sun and moon and other natural and seasonal patterns. These waves of energy are easily amplified, and where two lines of the Hartmann Net or Curry Grid cross, they create interference, or energy "hot spots". When such intense concentrations of energy interact with landscape features or man-made structures, such as buildings, roads, bridges or electricity pylons, they can create disturbances that affect health. The symptoms of geopathic stress include insomnia, exhaustion and depression. People with already high levels of stress are likely to be affected more noticeably.

We have found that the following placement reduces the effects of geopathic stress in most spaces. Pyrite and aventurine have a balancing, cleansing and protecting action, but you might like to use additional stones to suit the energy dynamics of your space. Use your intuition or dowse for the crystals that might be appropriate.

Pyrite × 4

Aventurine × 4

1 Locate the direction north in relation to the room or area you would like to improve. Place one pyrite crystal at each of the cardinal directions (north, south, east and west), as near to the ground as possible.

2 Place one aventurine crystal at each of the intermediate directions (north-west, north-east, south-east and south-west).

3 Leave the crystals in place for as long as you wish. You will need to cleanse them every day for the first week, and then weekly. You may like to change the type of crystal you use at regular intervals while you live in that space. Use your intuition to find the right stone.

N

W

E

S

CHOOSING A PERSONAL CRYSTAL

Geopathic stress can affect you wherever you go. And though cleansing a space you spend a lot of time in is certainly worthwhile, it will not offer relief outside that space. Wearing crystals or keeping a stone about your person is the most effective way to reduce problems when you are away from your protected space. It's best to dowse or use your intuition to find a crystal to protect you from geopathic stress. Your personal needs are unique to you, and any type of crystal can be supportive.

We have found these crystals effective against geopathic stress: black tourmaline, haematite, pyrite, copper, aquamarine, turquoise.

PLANETARY CONSCIOUSNESS

Only in the last 60 years has mankind had a view of the Earth from beyond our atmosphere. The vision of our fragile home floating in black space has triggered a sense of individual responsibility and a fear of destruction far beyond the experiences of our ancestors.

Emergent research into network theory, deep ecology and chaos theory has begun to affirm what ancient peoples suspected all along: that we are all ineluctably bound into an integrated energetic system. Thus, every being on Earth responds, albeit minutely and usually imperceptibly, to tides: not just those of weather, climate and magnetic field, but also of the emotions of fellow beings. Recent surveys have even shown a correlation between fluctuations in the Earth's magnetic field and large-scale human events. The concept of Gaia, or self-aware planetary consciousness, is a modern vision of what our ancestors understood as the Goddess of the Earth, origin and sustainer of life. The net opposite can help increase our awareness of how far our lives and our planet are interconnected.

RESONATING TOGETHER

The phenomenon of "phase transition" offers insight into how the connectivity of everything on the planet contributes to evolution. It also explains why a small act can have a wide impact. When a small proportion (around 1 per cent) of a community of individuals (molecules, people, emotions, ideas) begin to act in concert, the remaining 99 per cent of the community, no matter how chaotic and random their activities, quickly take up the pattern, forming a new state. Crystal formation is an example – once a coherent lattice is established, every atom falls into place around the template. The new state bears little resemblance to its components, and is more stable and efficient.

This net will stabilize your energies if they have been rocked by circumstance, and resolve feelings of insecurity, isolation or disconnection from life. It creates a quiet space within which priorities make themselves clear and important issues are not swamped by illusory concerns. Labradorite neutralizes external energetic pressures, whether human or environmental, while Herkimer diamond clarifies thoughts. The green cloth creates a balance so that no single energy encroaches on another.

Labradorite × 9

Black tourmaline × 1 (optional)

Herkimer diamond × 1

1 Spread out a green cloth on the floor. You may also like to light the room with a green-coloured light-bulb, or spend a moment before you begin visualizing yourself inhaling green-coloured air.

2 Position one labradorite so that when you lie down it is just above the top of your head. Place two more labradorites just below where each foot will be.

3 Place three labradorites along each side of your body, spacing them evenly apart. If you feel a particular need for grounding, you can place a black tourmaline on the midline of your body, below your feet.

4 Lie down and settle yourself within the energy net. Place the Herkimer diamond on the centre of your brow, then close your eyes and just relax.

5 After 4–5 minutes take a few deep breaths, stretch your fingers and toes and climb out of the crystal net, remembering to remove the crystal from your brow.

6 Cleanse the crystals and relax for a while before you resume normal activity. Repeat as often as required.

ENVIRONMENTAL TOXICITY

These days many of us worry about the impact of different man-made chemicals both on the environment and on ourselves. Airborne pollutants, particularly petrol and diesel fumes, are common to all cities, while the countryside is affected by the use of crop sprays and fertilizers. In the home we are exposed to a cocktail of chemicals from cleaning products, and toxins that evaporate from man-made fibres, furniture and building materials. Even the soil and seeds that produce our food are treated before and after growing with chemicals to impede the growth of weeds and increase crop yield. Preservatives and additives in processed food and in food packaging add yet more to our chemical exposure.

An overload of these pollutants may affect the systems of the body in various ways. Problems can include weakness in the immune system, sleep difficulties, behavioural changes, asthma, eczema and chronic fatigue. The crystal and visualization techniques here help the subtle bodies to cleanse themselves of unwanted substances and initiate deep healing.

SACRAL CHAKRA TEMPLATE

This simple layout balances all aspects of the sacral chakra. This chakra's associated functions include detoxification and the release of tension. A healthy sacral chakra will also encourage flexibility of mental processes, and relaxation.

1 Select three stones of the same type from the following: moonstone, rose quartz, lapis lazuli, aquamarine, sugilite, amethyst or charoite. You will also need three clear quartz crystals.

2 Lie down and place the quartz crystals (points directed toward your feet) between your navel and pubic bone in a downward-pointing triangle.

3 Place the three other stones in an arc, with the central, lowest stone placed on your pubic bone. Relax for 5–6 minutes before getting up. This can be repeated at regular intervals – once a week or once a month.

CLEANSING VISUALIZATION

You can carry out this straightforward visualization whenever and wherever you need to clear the influence of harmful energy, such as pollutants, from your body. Using this technique to release a build-up of negative emotion is particularly refreshing.

1 Settle yourself into a comfortable position, whether lying down, sitting or standing. For two or three breaths, allow yourself to relax as you exhale.

2 Imagine that you have a tap (faucet) on each foot. On your next out-breath, visualize emotions, stresses or toxins being released from the taps on your feet, down into the planet.

3 Imagine that the Earth transforms the harmful energy you release into positive energy, and transports it to where it is needed. Visualize the energy you discard becoming healing energy for the planet and for other beings.

4 With each out-breath continue releasing what you no longer need, knowing that the energy will be used for the benefit of others.

5 After 4–5 minutes allow the visualization to fade, and bring your awareness back to your body. Get up slowly. Repeat as often as required.

FINDING YOUR CENTRE

The crystal healing technique on the opposite page symbolically and actually reintegrates us into our surroundings. It derives from the Buddhist mandala and Native American medicine wheel. In both traditions, symmetrical patterns act as symbolic "maps" of the cosmos, and in the exercise, opposite, your body becomes the centre of the pattern. As you place stones in an arrangement around yourself, you connect your body with the four cardinal directions (north, south, east and west) and three levels of the cosmos (below, here and above). The simplicity of the act belies the profound experience it often creates for the participant.

STONE CIRCLES AND ALIGNMENTS

Arrangements of stones that mark and represent the relationship between visible phenomena are among the earliest expressions of human intellect. The stone circles and alignments of the Neolithic Atlantic cultures are the earliest known examples of the symbolic mapping of our place in the universe. Later we find similar ideas developing into the geometrics of sacred architecture, Chinese Feng Shui, Indian Vaastu Shastra, the mandala constructions of Buddhist cultures and the North American medicine wheels. These arrangements of stone symbolically anchor the relationship between human existence and cosmic order. The constructions provide us with spiritual "maps" that help to site us physically and, more importantly, psychically in our landscape and universe.

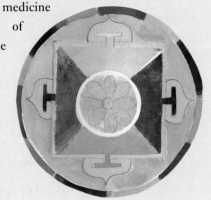

This technique can be used whenever you feel uncomfortable with your place in the world. Use an intuitive selection of stones and work in a large, open space if you can. But even if space is limited, the technique will be effective.

1 Clear an open space in the centre of the room or the space you are using for this exercise. Place your collection of crystals where you can see them all. Make an intention – to balance your internal energy with the energy of the elements around you. Quickly and intuitively select six or seven crystals. Keep conscious decision-making out of the process; let your eye and hand choose stones that attract your attention. Tidy away the unselected stones.

2 Stand in the centre of the space with your eyes closed or downcast, then slowly turn round in a circle on that spot. After two or three circles, you will notice that one direction feels more comfortable, or "right" (the actual compass designation is irrelevant). Place a chair to face in this direction.

3 From your chosen crystals, quickly and intuitively place four stones on the ground: in front, behind, to the left and to the right of the chair. Place the stones as far from the chair as possible within the space you have.

4 Place a fifth stone beneath the chair. Choose a sixth stone (and a seventh stone if you selected it in step 1), and hold them in your hands.

5 Sit on the chair with your eyes closed and relax. Maintain a relaxed awareness of your position in relation to the stones. Focus your attention on the space you occupy and the pattern of stones.

6 Remain in this alert but quiet state for 5–10 minutes. You may feel shifts in your perception and awareness as subtle energetic readjustments occur. When you feel ready, open your eyes and collect up the crystals.

7 Notice in the hours and days that follow whether any simple interpretations emerge from your intuitive choices of stone and placement. At the most fundamental level, the stone behind the chair represents the past; the stone in front, the future; to the left, your emotions; to the right, ideas; underneath the chair, what sustains you; and in your hands, your values and goals. Repeat this exercise whenever you feel disconnected from the world.

CRYSTAL DIRECTORY

This directory provides a concise survey of some of the many crystals and minerals that you are likely to come across, including some of the more unusual and fashionable minerals that are on the market. For ease of identification, stones are in colour groupings. This also lets you see how stones of similar appearance can have different qualities and effects.

It is an oversimplification to state that each stone has a specific use in terms of medical conditions, emotional well-being or spiritual advancement. The interaction of crystal and human energy systems is much more complex and individual than that. The information given here is a broad outline intended to give you a sense of each stone's possibilities.

FLINT
Formed from organic silicates in prehistoric seas. Early man used its natural sharp edges to make tools. Encourages dexterity, repairs, protects from harm.

AUGITE
A common pyroxene mineral forming long, lustrous black crystals. Has a bright, fast-moving energy that brings strength, boosts motivation, swiftly re-orients and speeds up mental processes.

NUUMMITE
Ancient metamorphic rock from Greenland, heavy, dense black with a sprinkling of refractive crystals. Promotes awareness of the passage of time and encourages patience, eases transformation.

SILVER
Found in its rare native form as tangled fibres, sheets or sometimes pebbles. Cooling; eases energy flow in all systems. Encourages inner quiet, protects from harmful influences.

JET
Fossilized wood from prehistoric forests. Very light and easily worked. Quietening, calming, gently grounding and stabilizing, boosts energy flow, widens perception.

METEORITE
Most commonly fragments of iron and nickel. Each meteorite has its own character. Energizes, stimulates new levels of awareness and inspiration. Links you to cosmic time.

ONYX
Black-and-white banded chalcedony quartz. Calms extremes of emotion, creates objectivity. Introspective effect can be somewhat sombre if the energy is not well grounded. Expanding and cleansing.

TEKTITE
Family of glasses created by meteoric impacts found around the world. Fiery and transformative, encourages re-evaluation and realistic solutions. May be grounding or activating depending on the source.

BRONZITE

Brown and gold with scintillating reflective surfaces and a soft, silky sheen. Protective, comforting. Integrates different levels of energy in the body, may enhance creativity.

FULGERITE

Silica sand fused into branch-like tubes by lightning strikes. Its highly charged energy is useful in counteracting rigidity. Promotes new ideas, inspiration, transformation.

LIMONITE

Soft, earthy aggregations of iron minerals, formed through the evaporation of water in hot desert conditions. Powerful earth energy, stimulates, balances physicality and links you to the energies of the planet.

STAUROLITE

Twinned crystals that form a cross shape, known as "fairy crosses". Calms and quietens the body. Useful for insomnia and decision-making. Focuses ideas, aids self-confidence.

VESUVIANITE

Also known as idocrase. Most often brown-green, vesuvianite's long, brittle blade-like crystals have a square cross-section. Offers opportunity to view things in new ways, in order to locate new solutions.

IRON QUARTZ

Rock crystal whose high iron content turns the stone opaque brick-red, translucent orange (tangerine quartz) or yellow (golden healer). Cleanses, energizes, focuses.

CHIASTOLITE

Andalusite crystals whose impurities form a distinctive cross shape when cut into cross-sections and polished. Protects from fear, brings equilibrium and poise.

HALITE

Salt precipitated from the evaporation of ancient oceans, commonly known as "rock salt". Soft and water-soluble, halite cleanses space and neutralizes negative energy.

PETRIFIED WOOD

Fossilized ancient trees where organic compounds are replaced by jasper, chalcedony and opal. Strengthens physical structures, brings flexibility, patience, perseverance, broadens perception.

TIGER'S EYE

Has characteristic reflective, silky bands of yellow and brown with blue and green. Encourages energy movement and sociability, supports practical activity. Increases confidence and clarity of thought.

EUDIALITE

A "new" mineral with a dynamic interpenetrating pattern of red, pink, green and black. Energizes, grounds and motivates, particularly strengthens the heart chakra.

RED GRANITE

A coarse, hard, large-crystalled rock that helps to integrate and unify different systems and subtle levels of the body. Energizing and stabilizing, it anchors healing processes and speeds recovery from stress.

147

RUBY IN ZOISITE

Found in igneous rocks. Attractive green varieties from Africa contain red and black granules of ruby. The combination of red and green makes this crystal useful both for calming over-active states and for stimulating new activity.

SPINEL

Occurs as small, thorn-like, red crystals with similar activating, energizing qualities to garnet. Focuses healing deep into the body, to stimulate the movement of stagnant energy.

ZINCITE

Manufactured from zinc-smelting processes; glassy with brilliant colouration. Very heavy, often appears to have been extruded. Stimulates, encourages new syntheses of energy and ideas.

ARAGONITE

The same mineral as chalk and calcite, but formed at higher temperatures. Usually columnar and six-sided, often found in radial clusters. Promotes clarity and invention, encourages study and discipline.

SARDONYX

Distinctively banded carnelian with orange, brown and white layers. Has the same gently healing qualities as carnelian, but, as its appearance suggests, also promotes orderly discovery and repair of damaged energies.

GOLD

The most precious of metals, remains untarnished and softly radiant for years. Rare, but small nuggets and grains can sometimes be found with quartz crystals. Soothing, amplifying and purifying, detoxifies and speeds healing processes.

MOOKAITE

Sedimentary, quartz-based stone from northern Australia identified by soft areas of earthy colours: reds, browns, purples, yellows and creams. Soothing, brings a practical and grounded confidence.

TOPAZ

An ancient gemstone, hard but brittle. Yellow or golden but may also be clear, pink or blue (the latter two are often heat-treated). Healing focus is on personal power, confidence and relaxation.

HELIODOR

Yellow or green-yellow variety of beryl. Has a light, bright, cleansing energy. Especially soothing to the nerves and emotions, a useful stone if you have a demanding job.

SEPTARIAN NODULE

Concretions of mud and rocks bound by calcite, aragonite and quartz into discrete cell-like shapes. Helps you find hidden creative potential. Unifies disparate and fragmented elements.

SULPHUR

Found near volcanic activity and hot springs, usually as crusts of powdery crystals. Extremely soft, requires delicate handling. Improves mental clarity and physical purification. Helps with detoxification.

BRAZILIANITE

A "new" and as yet rare yellow or green-yellow precious gemstone. Helps to determine what is appropriate and what should be avoided or removed from your life. Aids discrimination and judgment.

CHRYSOPRASE

A rich apple-green variety of chalcedony quartz found in thick veins between soft rocks. One of the best stones for encouraging peaceful sleep. Cleanses, calms, boosts creativity.

PRASE

Quartz coloured green by the presence of needle-like actinolite crystals. "Prasiolite" is heat-treated quartz, more transparent than natural prase. Liberates, unifies, brings awareness of the healing power of nature.

PREHNITE

Usually massive, translucent milky-green or yellow-green. Conveys a gentle action in order to dissolve false boundaries of time, space, mind or belief. Quietens, soothes, reassures, lifts worry and anxiety. Strengthens psychic skills.

SERAPHINITE

Form of chlorite with a soft lustre and radial clusters of silky shades of green and white. Clarifies personal direction, reveals spiritual inspiration and hidden aspects of your nature. Chlorite quartz has similar properties.

DIOPSIDE

Chrome diopside resembles green tourmaline, black diopside is often cut to make "black moonstone". Has a strong energy, harsher than tourmaline. Cuts through negativity and stress. Reaches the deepest layers of your being and restores energy balance.

DIOPTASE

Vivid, lustrous viridian crystals, found as small rectangular crystals in tight clusters. Stimulates and energizes, especially the heart chakra. Cleanses worn-out attitudes, encourages new starts, freshness and the expansion of your horizons.

EMERALD

Precious green variety of beryl with deep, rich colouration, translucent or transparent. Encourages truth, honesty, openness in relationships and harmony with the natural world. Calms, cleanses, quietens.

EPIDOTE

Similar appearance to tourmaline, brown-black or yellow-green. Anchoring and stabilizing. Encourages practical outlook and steadies the energy levels of the body. Aids the accumulation and control of strength.

149

HIDDENITE

Rare, delicate green form of spodumene.
Pink varieties are known as kunzite. Forms
transparent blades with striated
sides. Cooling and calming to
the heart chakra. Encourages
links with nature, and harmony
in your relationships.

IONA STONE

Also called "Connemara Marble" and
"Mermaid's Tears", this smooth,
pale green serpentine is found in
the Western Isles of Scotland
and in Ireland. Quietens
emotions and brings spiritual
comfort.

MOLDAVITE

Pitted and extruded dark green, translucent
tektite (see page 146), thought to have
originated in a meteor impact in central
Europe. Its lively energy
amplifies other stones,
expands consciousness,
develops spirituality.

MOSS AGATE

Chalcedony quartz with green and brown
inclusions resembling plant forms. Cooling and
opening, helps to relax and release
restriction and increase the flow
of positive energies. "Tree
agate" is more opaque.

PERIDOT

Small, translucent, bright apple-green crystals
found in volcanic environments. Excellent
stone for cleansing stress from the
subtle bodies and detoxifying.
Protects from negative
influences. Gem-quality
variety of mineral olivine.

SERPENTINE

Olivine-rich metamorphic rock with
characteristic smooth and slippery feel. Comes
in many colours (green is common), often has
sinuous patterning. Calming,
stabilizing, stimulates
energy flow and heightens
awareness.

SPHENE

Also known as titanite. Dull, olive-green,
wedge-shaped crystals. Reveals new paths and
aids exploration of them, brings insight through
different perspectives.
Promotes clarity of mind
and problem-solving, and
balances emotions.

STICHTITE

A purple mineral often seen with green
serpentine, a combination known as
"Atlantisite". Intense colour stimulates
awareness and focuses
attention. Aligns subtle
energy and clears the
deep channels of the aura.

VERDELITE

Green varieties of tourmaline that can be
distinguished from similar stones by their
changing colour when viewed at different
angles. Balances the heart
chakra, relaxes and aligns.
Reduces vulnerability.

CHRYSOCOLLA

A stunning mineral with varying shades of
turquoise, blue, green and red-brown. Can be
soft and powdery or intergrown with quartz.
Eases emotional expression,
improves communication skills,
enhances creativity.

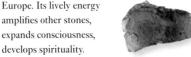

HEMIMORPHITE

Found with zinc and lead ore. Has many forms and colours but is frequently a milkily opaque, turquoise blue with silky luminescence. Protects from damaging influences, strengthens life-energy. Calming, cooling.

LARIMAR

Rare form of the mineral pectolite, larimar has turquoise-blue areas within irregular milky-white cells. Expands consciousness, encourages tolerance and equanimity. Lifts feelings of restriction and spiritual oppression.

SHATTUCKITE (PLANCHEITE)

A copper mineral also known as plancheite, similar to chrysocolla but with more dark flecks and often areas of deeper blue. Disengages you from external manipulation. Activates subtle levels of protection. Speeds flow of information and energy.

SMITHSONITE

A zinc ore also known as calamine, found in crusts and rounded aggregates, may be blue, green or white. Brings disparate energies into harmony and speeds the removal of unnecessary factors. Unifies, focuses the mind, improves communication.

ANGELITE

A pale blue, massive variety of anhydrite, which forms when water evaporates from gypsum. Soothes, quietens, instils peace and reduces stress. Can be used for enhancing subtle communication.

APATITE

Phosphate-rich mineral found especially in sedimentary conditions where it forms from organic decay. Blue and green varieties are common, yellow is rarer. Brings structure, organization of energies, flexibility and strength.

BLUE QUARTZ

Rare, usually massive, occasionally found as transparent crystals. Calming, protects from chaotic influences. Strengthens your body by increasing efficiency of internal communication. Excellent meditation aid.

CELESTITE

Soft, heavy, large, blue, chisel-shaped crystals often found as geodes. Uplifting, instils spiritual peace and a deep contentment that may even be blissful. Brings a sense of communication and communion with spiritual aspects of life.

TANZANITE

Rare gem-quality form of zoisite, the blue–violet colour varies according to density and viewing angle. Activates, transmutes, focuses balancing and healing energy wherever it is placed. Stimulates intuition and perception.

AZURITE

Powder-blue nodules, crusts or crystals with a lustrous, electric-blue sheen. Oxidizes to malachite. A copper ore, it speeds mental processes, especially access to buried memories. Excellent for intuitive insight.

151

COVELLITE

Also known as covelline or indigo copper. A soft, heavy, brittle mineral with a metallic, deep blue sheen. A combination of copper and sulphur, covellite cleanses, eases transformation, promotes intuitive insights.

DUMORTIERITE

Blue or violet-blue often speckled with brown, usually found in massive form. Combines cooling flow with practical focus. Useful for emotional balance, patience and understanding. More grounding than many blue stones.

INDICOLITE

Rare blue variety of tourmaline, whose colour ranges from blue-green to shades of violet. Encourages communication, detached awareness, and the clear expression of will.

KYANITE

Thin, blade-like, blue, black or green crystals, sometimes of gem quality, often radiating out from a base in striated and compacted leaves. Shifts energy, removes blocks, clears communication channels.

AMETRINE

Amethyst with areas of golden citrine, usually found as transparent, tumbled stones. The combination is excellent for maintaining mental balance, calm, clarity and rationality. Reduces nervous tension and anxiety.

CHAROITE

A striking violet stone from Siberia featuring smudged, swirling, intermixed patterns of black, pink or clear stone. Helps to integrate different states, improves flexibility. Soothing and facilitates spiritual alignment.

IOLITE

Also known as water sapphire, translucent, violet-blue crystal with blue-grey or brown tints. Often found in unpolished pieces, sometimes of gem quality. Brings clarity of thought in decision-making, refines feelings.

SCAPOLITE

The striking vibrant purple variety is rarer than the golden form of this stone. Can be found as crystals similar to beryl, and as cut gemstones. Cleanses spiritual energies, develops independence and aligns purpose.

SUGILITE

Also known as lavulite or royal azel, opaque, dark violet or purple rock shading to black (beware of dyed imitations). Aids co-ordination, and integration, boosts confidence in your spiritual identity.

PRASIOLITE

A new, artificially treated amethyst, usually green, violet-green, or pale and transparent. Transmutes subtle levels so that they can be understood. Adds empathy and understanding to transpersonal awareness.

152

PURPURITE

Opaque with a soft, silky sheen of violet fibres. Soft, so rarely tumbled. Knits together and soothes disparate energies. Encourages nutrient absorption and feelings of contentment and ease.

LEPIDOLITE

Mica coloured pink, or violet and pink, by lithium. May be found as pinkish tumbles or more intensely coloured crystals. Boosts self-awareness, protects, releases tension and doubt.

MORGANITE

Rare, valuable variety of beryl. Gem-quality morganite is transparent, pale pink. Lower grades look similar to rose quartz and milky quartz. Releases emotional pain and reduces aggravation regardless of the source.

PETALITE

A rare clear, grey or pink mineral of lithium also known as castorite, used for creating ceramics at high temperature. Associated with transformation and subtle levels of being. Transcends, unifies, purifies.

RUBELLITE

A pink or red variety of tourmaline. Good-quality rubellite is cut into gemstones while lower grades are translucent, dark and opaque. Darker shades activate and stimulate; paler shades calm and clarify. Increases confidence and creativity.

THULITE

A variety of zoisite coloured pink or red by manganese, found in massive form, slightly striated and opaque. Solidly grounds, brings awareness of your role in relation to the cosmos. Encourages acceptance, practicality and constancy.

ASTROPHYLLITE

Warm-brown or red columnar crystals in star-like needle clusters, sourced from Russia. Metallic lustre gives a subtle play of light. Usually embedded in amphibole and mica with zircon. Revealing, shifts energy, activates.

AZEZTULITE

Trademarked name for a low-density milky quartz from North Carolina, USA, that contains large quantities of gas and water bubbles. Same properties as quartz, but more activating. Encourages change and detachment from the mundane.

BRANDBERG QUARTZ

Exceptionally clear quartz from Namibia, shows distinct clouds of amethyst and colouration from smoky quartz. Unites the grounding, clarifying, illuminating qualities of the three quartz varieties it contains. Grounds spirituality.

HERKIMER DIAMOND

Small, brilliant, double-terminated quartz. Varieties from locations other than Herkimer may be coloured and have inclusions. Excellent for purification, detoxification, and, if the play of light is reflective enough, clarity of awareness.

153

MERLINITE

Blue-grey chalcedony often with subtle purple or white areas and branch-like inclusions of black. The blue encourages subtle levels of communication; the grey or white, access to the unknown; the black, practical exploration of subtle realms.

MILKY QUARTZ

Identical to clear quartz except that it contains small water or gas bubbles, causing the crystal to be opaque. Same qualities as clear quartz but gentler and more soothing. Relaxing, calming, clearing.

PHENAKITE

A rare beryllium silicate resembling quartz, usually clear, sometimes yellowish or pink. Combines the clearing qualities of quartz with the harmonizing nature of beryl. Attunes you to subtle realms.

TOURMALINE QUARTZ

Clear quartz inter-grown with tourmaline, usually black tourmaline. An ideal combination for strengthening the body and aura and protecting them from environmental negativity. Grounds, cleanses, integrates.

ZEOLITES

Group of related soft minerals, often found growing together as white, clear or colourless clusters on a common matrix. Most common are stilbite, okenite, heulandite and natrolite. Encourages harmony and co-operation.

DANBURITE

Light, sparkly, chisel-shaped crystals with striated sides. Very brilliant, usually clear. Often has a diamond-shaped cross-section. Activates energy, brightens mood, clarifies mind. Transforms and accelerates growth processes.

DIAMOND

Non-gem-quality crystals are available and more affordable. Encourages strength and invincibility. Rapidly realigns and cleanses all levels of the body. Can amplify subtle states of awareness.

ULEXITE

Known as the "TV stone", because its internal fibre-like crystals can transmit light and images from one side to another. Very soft. Removes energy blocks and shifts levels of awareness, promoting insight and inspiration.

ZIRCON

Various colours, crystals are often shiny red or brown, or opaque double pyramids. Often cut into gemstones. Similar to diamond in effect, though less forceful. Cleanses and transforms, reduces tendency to misunderstand.

CORAL

Mineralogically identical to calcite, chalk and aragonite. Usually found as beads or as polished sections of branch. The most valuable coral is red or pink. Supports physical structures, boosts courage and strength.

CHALCOPYRITE

A common ore of copper also known as peacock ore, because when weathered the mineral oxidizes into brilliant blues, violets and pinks. Stimulates and enlivens, yet simultaneously calms emotions and encourages flexibility of attitude.

MIXED JASPER

Variety of recombined microcrystalline quartz, coloured by various mineral impurities. Named acccording to appearance (such as orbicular or Dalmatian jasper). Stabilizes, encourages practical use of talents.

PARIBA TOURMALINE

Usually opaque with shades of turquoise and pink. This complementary combination of colours brings calm and peace, and gently protects delicate energies such as creativity and self-expression.

PEARL

Formed from thin layers of calcium carbonate and conchiolin within pearl oysters. Low grades are uneven or less lustrous – also be wary of synthetic pearls. Balances emotions, increases flexibility and tolerance.

ABALONE

Also known as paua, of the same organic origin as pearl and mother-of-pearl, but often more highly coloured and iridescent. Found as flat, polished pieces. Supports emotional stability, flexibility, creativity and artistic expression.

PIETERSITE

Resembles tiger's eye mixed with darker crystal in random swirls. Lustrous metallic browns, golds and blues. Eases rigidity, promotes flow of creativity, detaches you from negativity, anchors your energy during times of change.

SPECTROLITE

Often called rainbow moonstone, although it is in fact a different variety of feldspar. Fractured clear and white with a strong play of vivid blues. Deflects negativity, inspires, encourages purification and removal of unwanted energies.

TUGTUPITE

Newly available mineral from Russia and the Arctic regions. Pink, cream and black areas look similar to rhodonite but are more granular and less evenly coloured. Opens and balances heart chakra and self-awareness. Helps you put spiritual states to practical use.

UNAKITE

Opaque mix of feldspar, quartz and epidote that resembles granite, with distinct areas of light green and pink. Resolves conflict, balances emotions, encourages detachment from worry.

WATERMELON TOURMALINE

Named for its pink or red core surrounded by outer layers of green. Found as polished slices but also tumbles and natural crystals. Protects, restores, relaxes – an ideal balancer for the heart chakra.

GLOSSARY

AGATE – banded quartz composed of varying degrees of microcrystalline chalcedony, opal and terminated quartz.

ASTERISM – a star-shaped light appearing on a crystal's surface, caused by internal microcrystals.

AURA – electromagnetic field surrounding an animate or inanimate object.

BODY – here, all aspects of individual energy, both physical and subtle. The term "physical body" is used to refer to your anatomy.

CENTRING – process and techniques that focus awareness on the present, creating calm alertness.

CHAKRA – a spinning focus of subtle energy within or around the body that regulates or manifests some aspect of consciousness.

CRYSTAL – a mineral in its most stable state, exhibiting regular geometric planes and faces that reflect its internal atomic structure.

ELEMENT – an indivisible chemical constituent of matter. Elements combine to create compounds, which create minerals, which create crystals.

ENERGY – the inherent pattern or vibration that creates phenomena in the universe. Displays electromagnetic properties. "Subtle energy" is a fine level of energy interaction sensed or intuited by your awareness, undetectable by scientific method.

GEMSTONE – a worked and polished mineral found in jewelry.

GROUNDING – used to describe processes and techniques that anchor and stabilize body energy, preventing and releasing excess build-up of unnecessary or unwanted influences.

IGNEOUS – used to describe rock produced deep in the earth by volcanic or magnetic heat.

INCLUSION – small amount of water, gas or another mineral contained within a crystal.

LATTICE – the regular atomic structure within a crystal.

LAYOUT – a pattern of crystals placed on or around the body for healing.

MASSIVE – a rock or mineral exhibiting no clear crystalline structure.

MERIDIAN - a fine energy channel that usually runs close to the surface of the skin; meridians regulate the flow of life-energy (also known as *chi* or *prana*) around the body.

METAMORPHIC – used to describe a rock whose structure was altered by heat or pressure.

MINERAL – a compound that can be crystalline or non-crystalline. All crystals are minerals; not all minerals have a crystalline form.

NET – a particular technique that "catches" a specific type of universal energy and concentrates it around the person being healed. Devised by Simon and Sue Lilly.

SEDIMENTARY – used to describe dust from eroded, weathered rock and/or organic matter compressed over time under oceans to form new rock.

STRIATION – parallel grooves upon crystal faces, usually along the main axis.

SUBTLE BODIES – layers of the body's aura defined by function (emotional, mental, and so on).

TERMINATION – the natural point, apex or tip of a crystal's growth.

TUMBLING – process of smoothing minerals or crystals to produce "tumbled" stones. The stones are rotated over several days in a drum in which they are mixed with metal shot or other items.

FURTHER READING

Geinger, Michael, *Crystal Power, Crystal Healing*. Cassell & Co, London, 1998

Gerber, Richard, *Vibrational Medicine*, Inner Traditions/ Bear & Company, Rochester VT (USA), 1988

Gurudas, *Gem Elixirs and Vibrational Healing 1*. Cassandra Press, Boulder CO, 1989

Hankin, Rosie (ed.), *Rocks, Crystals, Minerals*. New Burlington, London, 1998

Korbel, Petr and Novak, Milan, *The Complete Encyclopedia of Minerals*, Rebo, Lisse (Netherlands), 1999

Kourimsky, Dr. J., *The Illustrated Encyclopedia of Minerals and Rocks*. Aventinum, Prague, 1977

Lilly, Simon, *The Illustrated Elements of Crystal Healing*. HarperCollins/Element, London, 2000 & 2002

Lilly, Simon and Sue, *Crystal Doorways*. Capall Bann, Milverton (UK), 1997

Lilly, Simon and Sue, *The Essential Guide to Crystals*. Duncan Baird Publishers, London, 2010

Lilly, Sue, *Crystal Decoder*. Barrons, Hauppage NY, 2001

Lilly, Sue and Simon, *Colour Healing*. Lorenz, London, 2001

Robins, Don, *The Secret Language of Stone*. Rider, London, 1988

SELECTED TRAINING ASSOCIATIONS

The Academy of Melody Crystal Healing Instructors
www.taomchi.com

Affiliation of Crystal Healing Organizations (20 schools)
www.acho.co.uk

Crystal Academy of Advanced Healing Arts
www.webcrystalacademy.com

Crystal Healing Academy of Japan
www.chaj.jp

Crystal and Healing Federation
(7 schools)
www.crystalandhealing.com

Institute of Crystal & Gem Therapists
www.icgt.co.uk

INDEX

AUTHORS' ACKNOWLEDGMENTS

We would like to acknowledge the many students and course participants who have shown us the great benefits that can come from crystals and crystal healing.